DRUM™
essentials

Produced by
Musicians Resources International
423 Atlantic Ave. Ste. 3E Bklyn, NY 11217
P. 718.875.6353 F. 718.875.5586

Publisher/ Editor

Catherine Herrera

**Associate Publisher/
Creative Director**

Maria Casini

Mac Layout Artist

Ann Simon

Illustrations

Maria Casini

Advertising Sales

Catherine Herrera

Maria Casini

Special Thanks To

Chuck Silverman

Kelsey Smith

Jorge Bermudez

Karl Perazzo

Steve Houghton

David Levine

Raul Artiles

Mike DiDonna

Michelle Pewter

Kristin Pape

ISBN 0-9657167-1-6
ISSN 1093-572X

HOW TO USE THIS BOOK

Uses for the Manufacturers section include: Finding product sources and information, Ordering catalogs, Locating your nearest dealer(s), Customer service, Inquiring about endorsement programs, Getting information about upcoming clinic dates in your area, Clinic and event support programs, Employment opportunities, etc.

Uses for the Equipment services section include: Sourcing out new, used, and vintage dealers, Locating rental and cartage co.'s, Finding the best service, stock availability, and price. **Search out companies** who offer repair and refurbishing, services and supplies to help you preserve your favorite gear. **Source out** new potential dealers for your product line.

Uses for the Education section include: Sourcing out institutions, organizations and workshops to help you further your formal and recreational musical education. **Networking** with colleges, universities, music schools, and annual workshop event organizers for employment opportunities including teaching positions, clinics and workshop performances. **Finding** instructional and listening materials to help you open and expand your musical boundaries. **Source out** potential new business opportunities for retailers and manufactures within the education sector.

Uses for the Trade Section include: Sourcing out trade events for manufactures and retailers, as well as finding potential new advertising venues for your products and services. **Source out professional organizations,** and promotional services to help you advance your music career or business.

Uses for the Glossary and Coupon sections include: Familiarizing yourself with the names and origins of some of today's most popular and not so popular drums and percussion related instruments, with cross references to manufacturer sources. **Saving money** when ordering from generous companies who have agreed to give discounts to our readers. **Use them!**

Cont

Drums

World Percussion

Concert

Marching

Electronics

DRUMS

WORLD

CONCERT

MARCHING

ELECTRONICS

D R U M S

ACCESSORIES

Aquarian Accessories Corp. 800 473.0231

Cannon / Universal Percussion . . . 800.282.0110

Creative Projects, Ltd.
1281 Uluplii St., Kailua HI 96734
P: 808.262.2022 **F**: 808.262.3294
The Pad-L, a great warm up pad. The Padd is stand mountable. Call for info. **See Coupon Section for $avings.**

Danmar Percussion Prod. 714 756.8481

Doc's Proplugs 800.521.2982

Drum Ruggers 716.624.5273

Future Perc Percussion 310.281.9549

Gorilla Snot Products
1750 N. Orange Drive #202, Hollywood CA 90028
P: 818.753.0535 **F**:818.753.0232
Gripping aid made of pine tar resin. Never lose your sticks again.

Grover Pro Percussion 617.935.6200

Holz Ltd. Drum Specialities
827 South Edison, Salt Lake City UT 84111
P: 801.537.7333 **F:** 801.359.0969
The reinstatement clamp for drumhead porting systems. Drum ring that allows you to cut a hole in your bass drum hd & reinstate the perimeter of the hole. Stops head from cracking or splitting. Also drum hd cutter - cuts 9 different size holes in any head.

HQ Percussion Products 800.467.3335

Kent Drum Distributing Co. 800.446.7676

King Kong Kases 800.776.1525

LP Music Group
160 Belmont Ave., Garfield NJ 07026
P: 973.478.6903 **F:** 973.772.3568
Web: http://www.lpmusic.com
Cowbells, jingle rings, mounted tamborines, chimes, clamps, & assorted toys for your drumkit. Send $3 for Catalog. See inside cover & ad on pg 37.

L.T. Lug Lock Inc 800.981.7842

Master Beat 800.908.4377

Mechanical Music Corp. 847.398.5444

D R U M S

ACCESSORIES cont'd

Pad-A-Rug Industries 800.4321.Pad

Patterson Cable Snares 210.655.8435

Perkana Percussion 800.406.0402

Perussion Ergonomic Developers . 800.528.7332

Peter Englehart Metal Perc. 800.726.2279

Players / Duratech 800.817.0017

Pro Design Percussion 916.722.5027

Rhythm Tech 800.726.2279

Slobeat Industries 303.277.1017

Slug Percussion
PO Box 578306, Chicago IL 60657-8306
P: 312.432.0553 **F:** 312.432.0552
Product Line: Powerhead™, Beaters Tweek®
drumkey-clip, Batter Badge™ impact pads™,
Muffelt ™ drumhead dampeners. Send SASE
for catalog. See ad pg 9.

Sonor (USA) / HSS Inc. 800.446.6010

Spectrasound Perc. Prods. 818.764.7690

Striker Drum Co. 610.296.5554

Taos Drums
PO Box 1916 So. Santa Fe Rd., Taos NM 87571
P: 800.655.6786/ 505.758.6786 **F:** 505.758.9844
Native American drumsticks, shakers, & rattles.
All natural materials. Call for free catalog.

Trick Percussion Products 800.448.7425

Vic Firth, Inc. 617.326.3455

Yamaha Corp. of America 616.940.4900

ACOUSTICAL PANELS

Auralex Acoustics 800.95.Wedge

Clear-Sonic Mfg 800.888.6360

Drummers Helpers Inc. 800.95.Drum1

Silent Source 800.583.7174

D R U M S

CASES

A & S Flight & Road Case Co. 818.509.5920

Anvil Cases 800.359.2684

Beato 310.532.2671

Cabbage Cases 614.486.2495

Cac - Sac
35 Ashford Place, Yonkers NY 10701
P/F: 914.969.4661
Top quality leather gig bags. Guaranteed workmanship. Individually hand made. Repairs on
all bags. Call for catalog n/c.

Calzone Case Co. 800.243.5152

Case Co International 206.361.Case

Drumslinger / Tough Traveler Ltd. . .800.Go.Tough

Flight Form Cases, Inc. 800.657.1199

Hardcase / MBT Int'l 800.845.1922

Humes & Berg Mfg. Co. Inc. 219 397.1980

Hybrid / Discount Distributors 800.346.4638

Impact Industries 715.842.1651

Kart-A-Bag/ Div of Remin 800.423.9328

King Kong Kases
PO Box 6595, Ashland VA 23005
P: 804.798.7320/ 800.776.1525 **F:** 804.798.7323
Custom-built ATA style road cases. Light weight,
fiber cases. Hammond organ conversions,
drumdial. Call for catalog & price list N/C. **See
Coupon Section for $avings!**

Levy's Leather Ltd. 800.565.0203

LM Products 800.876.7651

Modern Case Co. 800.344.7027

On the Case Prod. 800.Case.102

Peavey Electronics Corp 601.483.5365

Porcaro Pro-Covers 310.532.2671

Pro Tec International 800.325.3455

D R U M S

C A S E S cont'd

Reunion Blues
2525 16th Street, San Francisco CA 94103
P: 415.861.7220 **F:** 415.861.7298
Quality leather gig bags. Call for free catalog.
Full repair available on bags.

Roadrunner Cases 213.770.4444

Music Industries 800.431.6699

Six Eight Bags 916.342.9282

SKB/ Freed International 305.378.1818

Striker Drum Co. 610.296.5554

Veiger Cases- Hungary 36.83.360.203

XL Specialty Percussion Inc.
16335-5 Lima Road, Huntertown IN 46748
P: 800.348.1012 **F:** 219.637.6354
Eml: xlspl@aol.com
Protechter cases - plastic molded drum, cymbal,
accessory cases. Lifetime warranty against
cracking. Pro endorsed. Call for free catalog.

C Y M B A L   A C C E S S O R I E S

Abel Industries 307.789.6909

Aquarian Accessories Corp. 800.473.0231

Buckaroo Cymbal Cleaner 508.668.9444

Cymbal Buddy Kit / Gray West ...888.763.5460

Cymbal Crown / Big Bang Dist. 818.727.1127

Groove Juice 864.599.1651

HQ Percussion Products 800.467.3335

Paiste America 800 472.4783

Pro Design Percussion 916.722.5027

Resource (Kick N' Brass) 888.658.7046

Slobeat Industries 303.277.1017

Taw's Drum Works 216.835.1382

D R U M S

C Y M B A L S

Amati Percussion 847.520.9970

Bosphorus Turkish Cymbals 770.447.1047

Camber Cymbals 415.492.9600

Istanbul Cymbals/ Daito USA 407.339.7799

Meinl (USA)
PO Box 6595, Ashland VA 23005
P: 804.798.7320/ 800.776.1525 **F:** 804.798.7323
Call for catalog.

Paiste America 800.472.4783

Sabian, Ltd. 506.272.2019

Striker Drum Co. 610.296.5554

Turkish Cymbals- Turkey 90.212.642.8867

UFIP Earcrafted Cymbals
101 Bernoulli Circle,93030
P: 805.485.6999 / **F:** 805.485.1334
UFIP Class, Experience, Natural & Rough cymbals are "earcreated" by Italian artisans for a unique yet musical sound & performance.

Wuhan Cymbals 818.584.0232

Zildjian Cymbal Co. 617.871.2200

DAMPENERS & MUFFLERS

Danmar Percussion Prod. 714.756.8481

Husher Int'l, Ltd.
PO Box 71, Sayville NY 11782
P: 516.471.7275
Husher's design allows "real feel" response, bounce & tone with 90% less volume. Even brushes can be used. Be smart, Practice safe sound!
See ad pg. 9 & Coupon Section for $avings.

Physics Muffler/ GC Music 617.323.4154

Quiet Tone 908.431.2826

Slobeat Industries 303.277.1017

D R U M S

DAMPENERS cont'd

Slug Percussion
PO Box 578306, Chicago IL 60657-8306
P: 312.432.0553 **F:** 312.432.0552
Product Line: Muffelt™ drumhead dampeners.
Powerhead™, Beaters Tweek® drumkey-clip,
Batter Badge™ impact pads™, Send SASE for
catalog. See ad pg 9.

DRUM BUILDING SUPPLIES

Anderson International Trading ... 800.454.6270

Eames Co. 617.233.1404

JW Enterprises
10004 Edge Cutoff Rd., Hearne TX 77859
P/F: 409.589.2430
"ZOGS"- Nylon shoulder washers. Eliminate
drum rattle & maintain desired tuning. Call for
brochure. **See Coupon Section for $avings.**

Keller Products Inc. 603.627.7887

Kent Drum Distributing Co. 800.446.7676

Lee Custom Drum 209.928.3078

Modern Drum Shop 212.575.8893

Precision Drum Co. 914.962.4985

Super Gloss Drum Material 602.279.4041

Suraya 413.529.2319

Walker Drum Co. 303.682.1755

Zicko's Drum Co. 816.361.1195

DRUMSETS

Ayotte Drums 604 736.5411

Cannon / Universal Percussion ... 800.282.0110

CB Percussion / Kaman Music ... 800 647.2244

D R U M S

Drum Research- Germany 49.231.171.921

Drum Workshop, Inc.
101 Bernoulli Circle, Oxnard CA 93030
P: 805.485.6999 / 800.453.7867 **F:** 805.485.1334
Web: www.dwdrums.com
DW's world-famous drums, pedals, & hardware
combine state-of-the-art production techniques
with traditional handcraftsmanship. See ad pg 17.

Fibes Drums 512.416.9955

Gabriel Drums- Greece 30.1.2320.252

GMS Drum Company 516.293.4235

Gretsch Enterprises 912.748.1101

Grover Pro Percussion 617.935.6200

Juggs Percussion 305.594.3909

Lang Percussion 718.624.1825

Le Bihan - France 02.98.88.24.83

Le Soprano Drums - Italy 39.35.621894

Ludwig Industries 219.522.1675

Magnum Drums - Germany 49.5451.909.180

Mapex USA
PO Box 1360, Lavergne TN 37086-1360
P: 615.793.2050 **F:** 615.867.1424
Eml: mapex@concentric.com
While Mapex has a full range of drums &
hardware for beginners & professionals, their
Mars Pro kits & Black Panther snares offer
high-end quality & affordable pricing to the
midrange drummer. See ad pg 19.

Monolith Composite 905.689.6173

Noble & Cooley Co. 413.357.6321

Page Drums 619.320.5183

Palmetto Drum Co. 864.232.1726

Pearl Corp. 615.833.4477

Peavey Electronics Corp. 601.483.5365

D R U M S

D R U M S E T S   cont'd

PJL Drums / GMDI 770.300.0707

Premier Percussion USA, Inc 609.231.8825

REMO, Inc.
28101 Industry Drive, Valencia CA 91355
P: 805.294.5600 / 800.525.5134 **F:** 805.294.5700
Web: www.remousa.com
Remo offers a full range of drumsets & world percussion instruments. Also see ad pg 23.

Slingerland 615.871.4500

Sonor (USA) / HSS Inc. 800.446.6010

Stingray Percussion 561.848.4489

Sunlite Industrial Corp. 818.448.8018

Tama Drums/ Hoshino USA 215.638.8670

Taos Drums
PO Box 1916 So. Santa Fe Rd., Taos NM 87571
P: 800.655.6786/ 505.758.6786 **F:** 505.758.9844
High quality handcrafted Native American style drumset! Indigenous woods & natural hides. Professional hardware included Free Catalog. See ad pg 43.

The Clevelander Drum Co. 216.691.9152

Trick Percussion Products 800.448.7425

Trixon Drums- Germany 44.7731.918237

Yamaha Corp. of America 616 940.4900

Zicko's Drum Co. 816.361.1195

D R U M S E T S / C U S T O M

A.P. Boom Theory 206.850.8656

ADM Custom Drums 619.386.2001

African American Drum Co.
PO Box 4385, Arcata CA 95521
P: 707.668.4173 **F:** 707.668.4173
American maple drumsets designed to customer specs. 6, 8,10 ply shells. Bronze lugs. Free brochure. **See Coupon Section for $avings**

D R U M S

Baltimore Drum USA 800.301.Beat

Bison Drum Co. 708.459.1255

Bleifuss Handcrafted 619.460.3901

Chris Brady & Craftsmen
17 Stone Street, Armadale, Western Australia 6112
P: 61.8.9497.2212 **F:** 61.8.9497.2242
US Distributor: Woody Compton,c/o Sound Ideas
3215 NW 13th St., Gainsville, FL 32609.
P: 1.352.378.0192 F: 1.352.371.1791

D'Amico Drums 510.226.8700

G.C. Burger Drum Co./ Canada . . 519.974.4440

GVD Drums/ Canada 418.267.4565

Giannini Swiss Drums
PO Box 1547, Media PA 19063
P/F: 610.892.4742
Eml: duoselah@mindspring.com
High quality, high performance, precision per-
cussion instruments - in the Swiss tradition.
Dealer inquiries welcomed. See ad opposite pg.

Groove Music 905.627.5524

Heritage Drum Co. 205.533.5498

Honhegger Drums - Canada 819.459.3343

JC's Custom Drums 810.852.3660

Joe Montineri Custom Drums 860.645.6201

Kansas City Drumworks 816.471.3786

Kenner Drum Co. 606.635.5218

Keplinger Drum Co. 206.632.1714

Magstar Drums 508.747.3493

Mapleworks USA 410.203.0292

Obelisk Drums 403.236.9169

Orange County Drums & Perc. . . . 714.589.7308

Pork Pie Percussion 818.992.0783

RJS Custom Percussion 509.674.5337

D R U M S

Rocket Shells
5431 Auburn Blvd. #346, Sacramento CA 95841
P: 916.334.2234 **F:** 916.334.4310
Eml: rocket@cwia,net
"Composite Drum Technology". Complete line of
carbon fiber drums. Wide variety of sizes &
styles available. Catalog N/C.

Sleishman Drum Co./ Australia . . .61.026.009472

Spaun Drum Co. 818.914.9699

Striker Drum Co. 610.296.5554

Taos Drums
PO Box 1916 So. Santa Fe Rd., Taos NM 87571
P: 800.655.6786/ 505.758.6786 **F:** 505.758.9844
Highest quality handcrafted Native Amer. style
drumsets!. Log & stave construction kits, bass,
toms, snares, congas, tribal. Prof. hardware, full
customization. Free Catalog. See ad pg 43.

The Bearing Edge 770.967.8263

Wells Custom Drums / Canada . . . 519.753.6581

Wood Stock Drum Co.
1819 Industrial Drive, Wadena MN 56482
P/F: 218.631.2365 / **P:** 800.770 9254
Custom handcrafted drum kits. See Ad on pg 19.

DRUMSETS/ CUSTOM SNARES

Alto Ritmo - Italy 39.322.87760

Various Artist Percussion 209.255.7475

Drum Heaven 617.666.6616

US Custom Drums Ltd. 914.336.6671

Walker Drum Co. 303.682.1755

D R U M S

H A R D W A R E

Airlogic Percussion
9904 Running Brook Drive, Parma OH 44130
P: 216.888.8813 **F:** 216.888.8031
Pneumatic bass drum pedals with adjustable air
pressure and true-center to off-center cam settings.

Axis / Engineered Percussion
24416 S. Main St. #310, Carson CA 90745
P: 310.549.1171/ 800.457.3630 **F:** 310.549.7208
Complete line of Axis foot pedals & hi-hat stands
(incl. dble pedals, Axis-E Trigger pedals, Axis
Vortex drum stand- ltwt alum construction, flex
drum mtng system. Call for info & nearest dealer.

Bradical Drum Hardware 813.920.5669

Calac / Big Bang Distribution 818.727.1127

Cannon / Universal Percussion . . . 800.282.0110

Drum Workshop, Inc.
101 Bernoulli Circle, Oxnard CA 93030
P: 805 485.6999 / 800 453.7867 **F:**805 485.1334
Web: www.dwdrums.com
DW's world-famous drums, pedals, & hardware
combine state-of-the-art production techniques
w/ traditional handcraftsmanship. See ad pg 17.

Falicon Design 813.796.2468

Gemini Percussion Systems 800.205.8147

Gibralter / Kaman Music Corp 800.647.2244

GMS Drum Company 516.293.4235

Impact Industries 715.842.1651

JW Enterprise
10004 Edge Cutoff Rd., Hearne TX 77859
P: 409.589.2430 **F:** 409.589.2430
ZOGS- Nylon shoulder washers. Eliminate drum
rattle & maintain desired tuning. Call for
brochure. **See Coupon Section for $avings.**

Kent Drum Distributing Co. 800.446.7676

Mapex USA
1248 Heil Quaker Blvd. Lavergne TN 37086-1360
P: 615.793.2050 **F:** 615.867.1424
Eml: mapex@concentric.comMapex has a full
range of drum hardware for beginners & professionals. See ad pg19.

Drumming Essentials

Remo, Inc.
28101 Industry Dr.
Valencia, CA 91355
www.remousa.com

D R U M S

H A R D W A R E cont'd

Monolith Composite 905.689.6173

NADA Chair 800.722.2587

Pearl Corp. 615.833.4477

Peavey Electronics Corp. 601.483.5365

ROC-N-SOC 704.452.1736

Slingerland 615.871.4500

Sonor (USA) / HSS Inc. 800.446.6010

Sunlite Industrial Corp. 818.448.8018

Tama Drums/ Hoshino USA 215.638.8670

Yamaha Corp. of America 616.940.4900

H E A D S

Aquarian Accessories Corp. 800.473.0231

Attack/ Cannon Percussion 800.282.0110

D'Addario/ Evans Mfg.
595 Smith St., Farmingdale NY 11735
P: 516.439.3300 **F:** 516.439.3333
Genera, Rock, Hydraulic, Uno, Resonant & ST.
Tone control rings, EQ pads & patch.
See ad pg 21.

REMO, Inc.
28101 Industry Drive, Valencia CA 91355
P: 805.294.5600/ 800.525.5134 **F:** 805.294.5700
Web: www.remousa.com
Remo drumheads offer the highest quality &
widest variety of types, weights, sizes & sounds
for drumset, concert, marching & world perc.
See ad pg. 23.

Striker Drum Co. 610.296.5554

D R U M S

PRACTICE ACCESSORIES

Abel Industries 307 789.6909

Drum Sticky / Ethos Int'l 812.752.6848

HQ Percussion Products 800 467.3335

Jemm Company 303.296.1660

Power Wrist Builders
434 Corte De Rosa, San Jose CA 95120
P: 408 997.9560 / 800 645.6673 **F:** 408 997.9780
"The ultimate practice sticks" are designed to
increase drummer's wrist strength, agility, &
endurance. Alum. or brass. Free Catalog"

REMO, Inc.
28101 Industry Drive, Valencia CA 91355
P: 805.294.5600/ 800.525.5134 **F:** 805.294.5700
Web: www.remousa.com
Tunable Practice Pads. Also see ad pg 23.

RTOM Corp. 201.569.3603

Xymox Percussion 909.390.6995

STICKS

Agner Swiss Drumsticks 41.44.200.05

Ahead Sticks / Big Bang Dist. 818.727.1127

Aquarian Accessories Corp. 800.473.0231

Axis / Engineered Percussion
24416 S. Main St. #310, Carson CA 90745
P: 310.549.1171/ 800.457.3630 **F:** 310.549.7208
Drumsticks/ World sticks- Axis Whips - unique
combination, multi-percussion sticks. Virtually
unbreakable. Call for info & nearest dealer.

Ayotte Drums 604.736.5411

Back Bay / Kaman Music 800.647.2244

Cannon / Universal Percussion . . . 800.282.0110

Cappella Drumsticks 609.448.1153

Drummers Helpers Inc. 800.95.Drum1

Emmite Drumsticks / Canada 519.579.8197

STICKS cont'd

Flix / Big Bang Distribution 818.727.1127

JC's Drum Shop
43 Cliffwood Rd., Baltimore MD 21206
P: 410.661.7507 **F:** 410.661.3906
Handcrafted persimmon wood drum sticks &
bass drum beaters. 3 marching styles, concert &
drumset model.

Jopo Music / Diamond Tip 818.995.6208

Kent Drum Distributing Co. 800.446.7676

Kit Tools 888.Kit.Stic

Mainline Equipment 800.444.2288

Malletech 908.774.0088

Master Beat 800.908.4377

Mike Balter Mallets 847.541.5777

Peavey Electronics Corp. 601.483.5365

Players / Duratech 800.817.0017

Power Wrist Builders
1434 Corte De Rosa, San Jose CA 95120
P: 408.997.9560/ 800.645.6673 **F:** 408.997.9780
"The ultimate practice sticks" are designed to
increase drummer's wrist strength, agility, &
endurance. Alum. or brass. Free Catalog

Pro Design Percussion 916.722.5027

Pro-Mark Corp.
10707 Craighead Drive, Houston TX 77025
P: 800.822.1492 **F:** 713.669.8000
Eml: info@promark-stix.com
Full line of sticks, drum Corp & keyboard mallets,
& percussion accessories. Call for info.

Regal Tip (Calato Mfg)
4501 Hyde Park Blvd., Niagra Falls NY 14305
P: 716.285.3546/ 800.358.4590 **F:** 716.285.2710
Innovative Mfr. of the worlds most complete line of
sticks, brushes, mallets & perc. accessories. All
products mfr'd in-house at N   Falls location. Call
for free catalog.

Rim Shot 416.656.8462

D R U M S

STICKS cont'd

Slobeat Industries 303.277.1017

Tama Drums/ Hoshino USA 215.638.8670

Trick Percussion Products 800.448.7425

Trueline Drumstick Co. 802.485.4900

Vater Percussion, Inc. 617.767.1877

Verisonic Inc. 412.831.3343

Vic Firth, Inc.
65 Commerce Way, Dedham MA 02026
P: 617.326.3455 **F:** 617.326.1273
Full line of sticks & mallets for snare drum, timpani,
marching percussion & keyboard percussion.

DRUM TECHiNG

BEHiND THE SCENES

An Interview with Drum Tech Kelsey Smith

Q. What exactly does a Drum Tech do?

A. A drum techs job is to make sure an artists drum kit is up to show standards. Make sure it looks good, sounds good and is mechanically well maintained. You are there to support an artist by seeing to it that all he/she has to do is show up and play.

Q. What kinds of things should a tech know? Skills should they have?

A. A tech should know good drum maintenance including changing heads, fixing hardware problems, tuning & cleaning. They should also possess good communication and listening skills, be very responsible and have a great deal of patience because you never know what surprises may come up on the road.

Q. How does one get started as a tech?

A. Try to hook up with a local act that needs a tech. Offer your services. Be responsible and knowledgeable, and be willing to work for not much money at first and learn the ropes.

Q. How do you find work?

A. Mostly word of mouth. Once you get established then people usually call you.

Q. What are the hours like and what is the earning potential for a good tech?

A. Techs usually work about 8 hrs a day, with set up and load out. Depends how big the rig is. A tech can earn anywhere from $800 to $1200 a week, maybe more depending on experience and the gig.

Q. What do you enjoy about your job? Dislike?

A. Like any job it has its ups and downs. I enjoy traveling around the world and meeting new people wherever I go. Working with great musicians. It's a pretty easy gig when you get the hang of it. The downside is your not home a lot. Being on the road can be tiring especially when you have back to back gigs taking you to a new town every day, or those one to two day gigs, where you fly out of the country for one show and head back home again.

KELSEY SMiTH has been a professional drum tech for 10+yrs. He worked 8 yrs with the Neville Bros, & currently tours with George Howard & Al Jarreau.

Drum Essentials Tips for

TECH WANNABE'S

These tips may sound like simple common sense but they take a little extra time and effort   and sometimes get forgotten in the shuffle.

Remember: Organize and prioritize: Figure out what's the most important thing that needs to get done, do it and move on to the next thing.

Think Ahead: Always learn to anticipate potential problems before they occur. Think about the possible things that can go wrong, assume they will, and cover your bases. Whether its stocking enough sticks and heads, or having the right screws and enough duct tape, make sure you've got it covered.

Patience and Good Communication skills: Dealing with artists egos, managers, studios, union people, and artist relations reps, can all be trying at times. Learn to keep your cool. Deal with everyone you encounter with as much courtesy and professionalism as you would expect yourself. You may not always receive the same in return, but as corny as it sounds you'd be surprised how many more bees you get with honey . Good communication skills are key to getting what you want when you want it.

Be Appreciative: Always remember to thank everyone who helps make your job just a little bit easier. Especially endorsement companies and their AR reps, helpful retailers, and everyone else in between. Send them a thank you note, give them a thank you call, send them a tour shirt or maybe invite them to a show. They'll remember the gesture and always be there when you call on them again.

Time Management: Use your time wisely and responsibly. Whether your on stage setting up, or on personal down time, the bottom line is when your on the road, your always on call. Everything you do, effects your overall performance. Make sure you are where you are supposed to be, when your supposed to be and not distracted by people or problems you encounter on the road. Otherwise, guaranteed they'll send you packin'.

Being a drum tech can be lots of fun, but it is A JOB! and requires a great deal of responsibility. If you love music, drums and drumming, like to travel, meet new people and can deal with all the responsibilities that come along, then this might just be the gig for you.
OH, & DON'T FORGET TO TAKE DRUM ESSENTIALS!

W O R L D

ACCESS & SML PERCUSSION

Afena Akoma Inc. 800.98.Afena

Africa West 888.777.West

Afro Percussion 615.833.4477

Bailes African Drum Works
7816 Cryden Way, Forestville MD 20747
P: 800.861.Drum/ 301. 7364708 **F:** 301.736.7721
Web: BAILESADW@AOL.COM
See ad opposite pg.

Black Swamp Percussion 616.738.3190

Cannon / Universal Percussion . . . 216.755.6423

Caribbean Rhythms, Inc. 504.895.1589

Drum Spirit 520.282.3860

Final Chants Music Co. 800.554.3786

Fredrico Percussion 717.766.1332

Gon Bops 909.902.9489

India Street Percussion 423.378.5610

International Art & Sound . . . .800.555.9205 x 3013

International Percussion Imports . . 800.418.9793

JCR Percussion 718.293.6589

L.J. Percussion 800.536.7623

Lawton Percussion
1479 Brighton St., Arroyo Grande, CA 93420
P/ F: 805.473.9389
"Maru" natural gourd guiros, Cuban as well as new
"Bossa" thin lined guiro w/ bright, crisp sound!
"Banda Bros." shekeres, steel drums. Cases &
stands. **See Coupon Section for $avings**

LP Music
160 Belmont Ave., Garfield NJ 07026
P: 973.478.6903 **F:** 973.772.3568
Web: lpmusic.com
Full line of drum & percussion toys, hand percus-
sion & accessories. Call for catalog.

Lucinda Ellison Musical Instr. 615.449.6654

Mid East Mfg., Inc. 407.724.1477

Peter Englehart Metal Perc. 914.381.2279

ACCESS & SML PERC cont'd

Picante / Midco International 217.342.9211

Plugs-Perc 615.356.7050

Regal Tip (Calato Mfg) 716.285.3546

REMO, Inc.
28101 Industry Drive, Valencia CA 91355
P: 805.294.5600/ 800.525.5134 **F:** 805.294.5700
Web: www.remousa.com
Remo World Percussion includes, tambourines,
shakers & other hand perc. & accessories based
on native instruments from around the world.
Also see ad pg 23.

Rhythm Pick 818.710.8945

Rhythm Tech 914.636.6900

Rhythms 408.246.1002

Sabar - Germany 49.4203.810177

Skin on Skin 718.467.4110

Stick Drums 212.473.1315

The Overseas Connection 303.465.9585

Wright Hand Drum Co. 301.797.2067

C A S E S

Beato 310.532.2671

Buck Musical 215.345.9442

Gon Bops 909.902.9489

Humes & Berg Mfg. Co. Inc. 219.397.1980

Impact Industries 715.842.1651

JP Percussion Cases 714.373.2721

King Kong Kases 800.776.1525

LP Music
160 Belmont Ave., Garfield NJ 07026
P: 201.478.6903 **F:** 201.772.3568
Web: lpmusic.com
Selection of soft padded conga, bongo & timbale
bags. Also plastic molded conga cases.

CASES cont'd

On the Case Prod. 800.Case.102

Porcaro Pro-Covers 310.532.2671

Pro Tec International 800.325.3455

Six Eight Bags 916.342.9282

Small Dog Products
574 Boston Avenue, Medford MA 02155
P: 617.396.0662 **F:** 617.396.0712
Eml: cavallaro@biz.net or erinbliss@aol.com
Carry bags for ethnic drums. Wide range of sizes
& styles. Waterproof nylon or natural hemp w/
man-made shearling lining. Call for free catalog.
See ad pg 33 & **Coupon Section for $avings.**

Third Planet 818.337.4160

XL Specialty Percussion Inc.
16335-5 Lima Road, Huntertown IN 46748
P: 800.348.1012 **F:** 219.637.6354
Eml: xlspl@aol.com
Protechtor cases - Plastic molded bongo, conga,
accessory cases. Lifetime warranty against
cracking. Pro endorsed. Call for free catalog.

CYMBALS

Meinl (USA) 800.776.1525

Paiste America 800.472.4783

Sabian, Ltd. 506.272.2019

UFIP Earcrafted Cymbals
101 Bernoulli Circle, Oxnard CA 93030
P: 805.485.6999 **F:** 805.485.1334
UFIP Class, Experience, Natural & Rough cymbals are "earcreated" by Italian artisans for a
unique yet musical sound & performance.

Wuhan Cymbals 818.584.0232

Zildjian Cymbal Co. 617.871.2200

W O R L D

D I D G E R I D O O S

Blu Roo Ridgy -Didgeridoo
P.O. Box 142, Kwinana, Western Australia 6167
P: 61.9.527.7381 **F:** 61.9.527.7854
Specializing in the manufacture & distribution of
authentic Australian Aboriginal musical instru-
ments. U.S. warehouse P: 360.378.8323.
See Coupon Section.for $avings

Boongar Arts & Crafts Ltd.
PO Box 128, Yorkeys Knob Qld 4878
P: 011.61.70.93.8906 **F:** 011.61. 70.55.8196
Didjeridus handcrafted by aboriginal artist Boongar

Inma-Ku 773.279.0750

Knock on Wood 415.395.1317

E T H N I C   D R U M S

A.V. Drum Works
46 South Oxford St. #1, Brooklyn NY 11217
P: 718.722.7742 **F:** 718.722.7742
Handcrafted traditional Nyabunghi kete & funde
drums, also W. African djembe & djun djun.

Afena Akoma Inc.
250 Cumberland St. Ste. 203, Rochester NY 14605
P: 716.325.3790 / 800.98.Afena **F:** 716.325.6118
Eml: akoma@frontier.net **Web:** afenaakoma.com
Our products are authentic African instruments. Hand
chosen by 30 yr veteran percussionist & co. owner
Nana Collins. We carry only the best. Call for catalog.

Africa West
PO Box 10308, Wilmingon NC 28405
P: 910.762.3259/ 888.711.West **F:** 888.710.West
Web: AFRICAWEST@ aol.com
Traditional ceremonial rattles, tambourines,
gongs, shekeres, mbiras, balafons, & drums.
Handmade in West Africa. Call for catalog $5.
See Coupon Section for $avings!

African Tempo 888.848.9069

African & World Percussion Arts
115 S.Topanga Cnyn Blvd. Ste169, Topanga CA 90290
P: 800.733.drum/ 818.591.3111 **F:** 818.591.6756
Eml: drum1@pacificnet.net **Web:** www.pacificnet/~drum1
World percussion designs- Remo world percus-
sion- signature series. Djembes, Djun Djuns. . .
Drum videos, cds, instructional, drum circles.

E T H N I C D R U M S cont'd

Afro Percussion 615.833.4477

Afroton- Germany 069.9730.31.0

Akom La Engel- Germany 49.651.44951

All One Tribe Drums
PO Drawer N, Taos NM 87571
P: 800.442.Drum **F:** 505.751.0509
Handmade Native American drums. Indigenous
art. Patented (soft) handle. Superb quality, tone.
Custom bags, beaters, hangers. Free Brochure

Amani Drums & Perc.- Mexico . . .011.52.41527228

American Percussion Instr. 914.688.7520

B.D. Drums 206.463.6110

B.RAD Percussion 540.789.7369

Babylons End Percussion 606.689.5275

Barrelhouse Drum Co. 905.468.4668

Boemia 206.485.2484

Buck Musical Instrument Products
40 Sand Rd. New Britain PA 18901
P: 215.345.9442 **F:** 215.348.8761
Eml: MARTIAN @BELLATLANTIC<>NET
Mfr. of Bodhrans, Tar, Deff, Triangles, drums,
Native Amer. Ino drums, rattles, mouth bows,
flutes. cases, beaters, rawhide hds, Irish flutes,
All made in the USA. Catalog available $2.

Caribbean Rhythms, Inc.
P.O. Box 15861, New Orleans LA 70175
P: 504.895.1589 **F:** 504.822.8280
Only full line perc. source from the Caribbean;
tambora, conga, bongo, pleneras, bata, bomba,
& palo drums, gourd shekeres, shakers, guira,
claves, bells, chimes. Catalog $5. See online free.

Casablanca 412.247.3370

Doumbecks by Barb Lund
520 W. 6th Street, Bloomington IN 47404
P: 812.339.8476 / Beautiful to the eye & ear,
drums thrown on my potters wheel at my studio.
Stone Doumbeks are highly versatile handrums w/ a
wide variety of tones;deeper doun sound from ctr
to the ringing higher bek sound. Made of stoneware
w/goatskin hds & finished w/ decorative ribbons
& sashes. **See Coupon Section for $avings.**

E T H N I C   D R U M S   cont'd

Dr. Kwasi Percussion
201 N. Braddick Ave. Ste 8, Pittsburgh PA 15208
P: 412.241.2420 **F:** 412.241.2446
One of kind handmade custom & art drums. Own design, unlike any others. Repairs on all world perc. drums, reskining. See ad page 39.

Drum Brothers Drums
PO Box 678, Arlee MT 59821
P: 406.726.4444/ 800.325.1201 **F:** 406.726.4443
Eml: drumbros@montana.com
Web: http://www.montana.com/drumbros
See ad pg 39.

Earth Rhythms 501.253.6986

Earthshaking Percussion 404.624.3349

Earthtone Drums 707.824.9706

Elemental Design 207.785.2212

Everyone's Drumming
PO Box 361 Christian Sq., Putney VT 05346
P: 802.387.2249/ 800.326.0726 **F:** 802.387.2249
Web:http://www.musicsource/.com/everyone's.htm
African style hand drums, crafted in the USA. All hand drum repairs. Call for free Catalog.
See ad pg 39.

Fat Congas 805.969.6125

Final Chants Music Co. 800.554.3786

Fred Halpin 613.824.8798

Fredrico Percussion 717.766.1332

Full Circle Drums
148 San Marcos Trout Club, Sta Barbara CA 93105
P: 805.967.2541 **F:** 805.967.2541
Handmade ceramic Doumbec drums, 3 sizes to choose from. We also offer a tunable ceramic Djembec. Call for free catalog. **See Coupon Section for $avings.**

Gon Bops 909.902.9489

Grover Music Products 800.321.0556

Handsong Drums 408.684.1365

Hawk Dancing Studio 715.263.2756

ETHNIC DRUMS cont'd

Hermans Arts & Percussion
3822 Overton Manor Ln, Birmingham AL 35243
P: 205. 967.0559
I handcraft a variety of drums. Detailed inlay, 3D
carvings & natural heads. Give earthy looks & tribal
tones, that will make you H.A.P.I. See ad opposite pg.

India Percussion 914.679.4490

India Street Percussion 423.378.5610

Jag Drums 617.648.6456

JCR Percussion 718.293.6589

Joyful Vibrations 406.458.9729

Kooienga Drums 704.683.9177

L.J. Percussion
1631 NW 94th Street, Gainesville FL 32606
P: 352.331.8017/ 800.536.7623 **F:** 352.371.6557
Your best source for African drums, parts, accessories, repair services & world beat percussion
needs. Top quality djembes & ashikos.

Large Community Drum Co. 207.722.3654

Lark in the Morning 707.964.5569

Lawton Percussion
1479 Brighton St., Arroyo Grande CA 93420
P: 805.473.9389 **F:** 805.473.9389
"Maru" natural gourd guiros, Cuban as well as
new "Bossa" thin lined guiro w/ bright, crisp
sound! "Banda Bros." shekeres, steel drums.
Cases & stands. Free catalog. See ad pg. 33
& Coupon Section for $avings.

LP Music
160 Belmont Ave., Garfield NJ 07026
P: 973.478.6903 **F:** 973.772.3568
Web: lpmusic.com
Full line of prof. quality congas, bongos, timbales, as well as African & Brazilian style hand
drums. See ad. pg. 37 & inside front cover.

Matthew Congas 610.868.8733

Mid East Mfg., Inc. 407.724.1477

Moondance 406.777.1344

Moperc 819.828.3482

Mountain Rythym 250.353.2204

ETHNIC DRUMS cont'd

Original Clandou Rhythm 518.279.0684

Paul Aljian Drumworks 201.833.4550

Picante / Midco International 800.356.4326

PJ Drums & Percussion- Denmark . . 45.31.105.710

Raul / Midco International 800.356.4326

REMO, Inc.
28101 Industry Drive, Valencia CA 91355
P: 805.294.560 / 800.525.5134 **F:** 805.294.5700
Web: www.remousa.com
Remo World Percussion includes Djembes, Djun-Djuns, Congas, Surdos, Doumbeks, Bodhrans, & a variety of other hand drums. Also see ad pg 23.

Rhythm Fusion 408.423.2048

Rhythm Tech 800.726.2279

Rhythms
P: 408.246.1002 /888.Udu.Igbo **F:**408.246.8310
Leading instr. mfr offering the latest in Exotic Afro perc, for beginners, hobbyists, & professionals. Udu drums, bells, shakers, spcl effects & more. Call for free catalog.

Roundstone Musical Instr.- Ireland . . 353.95.35875

Sabar - Germany 49.4203.810177

Schlagwerk Klangobjekte - Germany .49.7162.6066

Smiling Woods 509.486.1053

Sol 415.468.4700

Spirit in the Wood 215.598.0188

Stick Drums 212.473.1315

Supercussion- Netherlands 31.20.6241225

Talking Drums, Inc. 910.273.7470

Taos Drums
PO Box 1916, So. Santa Fe Rd. Taos NM 87571
P: 505.758.3796/ 800.655.3786 **F:** 505.758.9844
Finest quality handcrafted Native American style drums. Full line: frame (singl/dbl), pow-wow, & conga styles. Extensive *hand-painted* designs. Free drumstick & catalog. Also: African djembes, ashikos & ashebes. See ad pg 43.

Tapo Rhythm and Music 800.877.9825

W O R L D

ETHNIC DRUMS cont'd

The Overseas Connection 800.766.6049

Timbre Drums 603.735.5609

Toca / Kaman Music Corp 800.647.2244

Traditional Rhythms 770.964.0963

Tribe of Kings
RR 1 Box 321, Andes NY 13731
P: 914.676.3395
Eml: atif@catskill.net
Web: http://members.aol.com/mudjam
The finest all handcrafted ceramic darboukas:
6"-18" heads. highfired, super resonant. Beautiful
workmanship, professional sound. See ad pg 43.

Tygart River Pottery
Rte 2 Box 168, Bellington WV 26250
P: 304.823.2459
Web: http://www.well.com/user/reid
See ad pg 41.

UDU Drum 518.634.2559

West Cliff Percussion 800.900.Drum

Woodstock Percussion 914.331.2450

World Drums 505.753.9253

Wright Hand Drum Co. 800.990.Hand

Zenobia Music 860.350.4339

HARDWARE

Afro Percussion 615.833.4477

Handsong Drums 408.684.1365

LP Music
160 Belmont Ave., Garfield NJ 07026
P: 973.478.6903 **F:** 973.772.3568
Web: lpmusic.com
Hvy duty stands avail. for congas, bongos, djembes. Variety of clamps & perc. tables. Also see ad
on pg. 37 & inside front cover. Call for catalog.

Toca / Kaman Music Corp 800.647.2244

W O R L D

H E A D S   &   S K I N S

Bailes African Drumworks 800.861.Drum

Altenburger Trommelfel- Germany . . . 49.3447.314010

Babylons End Percussion 606.689.5275

Buck Musical 215.345.9442

Emray
111 Kings Highway, Landing NJ 07850
P: 201.770.4730
Break resistant bongo heads. See ad opp. pg.

LP Music
160 Belmont Ave., Garfield NJ 07026
P: 973.478.6903 **F:** 973.772.3568
Web: lpmusic.com
Variety of mounted & flat skins. Also synthetic
replacement heads. Also see ad pg 37 & inside
front cover.

Original Clandou Rhythm 518.279.0684

REMO, Inc.
28101 Industry Drive, Valencia CA 91355
P: 805.294.5600/ 800.525.5134 **F:** 805.294.5700
Web: www.remousa.com
Remo drumheads offer the highest quality &
widest variety of types, weights, sizes & sounds
for world percussion, drumset, concert, & marching.
Also see ad pg 23.

United Rawhide
1644 North Ada St., Chicago IL 60622
P: 773.276.1177 **F:** 773.276.9535
Genuine calf & goat skin heads. See ad pg 47.

M A L L E T   P E R C U S S I O N

Hardwood Percussion 800.555.9205

Rhythmwood Slit Drums 800.568.2896

Tapo Rhythm and Music 800.877.9825

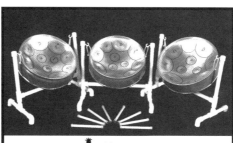

W O R L D

STEEL DRUMS

Calypso Steel Pan 914.331.7728

Fancy Pans
PO Box 8393, Santa Cruz CA 95061
P/F: 408.336.3537
We are THE mini pan specialists. Builders of a
full line of high quality, affordable steel drum
instruments, made in the USA. Instruction/ performance avail. See ad pg 47 & **Coupon
section for $avings**

Lawton Percussion
1479 Brighton St., Arroyo Grande CA 93420
P: 805.473.9389 **F:** 805.473.9389
"Maru" natural gourd guiros, Cuban as well as
new "Bossa" thin lined guiro w/ bright, crisp
sound! "Banda Bros." shekeres, steel drums.
cases & stands. Call for free catalog. See ad
pg 33 **& Coupon Section for $avings!**

Panyard, Inc. 330.745.3155

PR Percussion 800.722.0558

Trinidad & Tobago Instruments
144 Old St. Joseph Rd. Laventille, Trinidad & Tobago
P: 809.627.0185 **F:** 809.623.1634
Authentic quality steel drums. All sizes & types.
Made in Trinidad, mecca of the steel band world.
Accessories, aids, & services provided.

STICKS & MALLETS

Axis / Engineered Percussion
24416 S. Main St. #310, Carson CA 90745
P: 310.549.1171/ 800.457.3630 **F:** 310.549.7208
Drumsticks/ World sticks- Axis Whips - unique
combination, multi-percussion sticks. Virtually
unbreakable. Call for info & nearest dealer.

Buck Musical 215.345.9442

Inaki Sebastion Mallets 0034.43.33.12.41

Pro-Mark Corp. 800.822.1492

Regal Tip (Calato Mfg) 800.358.4590

Vater Percussion, Inc. 617.767.1877

Drum Circle Masochism

Excerpt from Jorge Bermudez' upcoming book "CONGA GROOVES"

Muchachos and muchachas, Drum Circles have become very popular in recent years. They give people of all ages an opportunity to meet others who are into community drumming and build musical friendships based on the mutual love for the big beat. I've had the privilege of meeting many of you who are into drum circles, and have witnessed your infectious enthusiasm for the beat. Unfortunately, I've also had to look at the condition of many of your hands. OUCH! If you keep bashing the hell out of your poor limbs they're going to wind up looking like old beat-up chicharones! (You know, those dried pork rings that hang in the potato chip section at the grocery stores.)

Por favor, people, patience with that pop. Remember it's skin and bones between you and that drum head. pounding your hands to a pulp, splitting your fingers will not make you a better player, It makes you vulnerable to infection, and it ain't pretty. Believe me, you don't want to meet my hand surgeon, Dr. Be-A -Man-You-Don't-Need- Anesthetics. Their weren't any teachers for us to

Drum Circle Masochism

study with in the Bay Area in the late 60's and early 70's so we just guessed at it. I developed bad habits and had to have and ugly growth removed from my index finger.

Put enough money aside so that you can take at least, a half dozen lessons on proper hand techniques. Your hands will be healthier and playing congas in a drum circle or anywhere else will become even more enjoyable.

A good teacher will increase your comfort and endurance without having to withstand needless pain. Let's have no more bleeding on the drums. . .

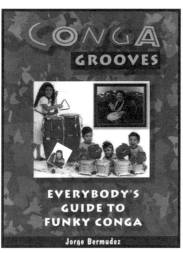

Look for Jorge's book in the spring of 1998

CONCERT

ACCESSORIES & SML PERC

Black Swamp Percussion 616.738.3190

Drum Dial Inc. 520.578.8975

Equilibrium 313.426.5814

Gambal Mfg.
PO Box 452, Chinchilla PA 18410-0452
P: 717.457.8903 **F:** 717.457.8906
Eml: gambalmlts@aol.com
Mallets for keyboard, concert bass & gongs,
toms & bass. Brushes, drum keys, cymbal
straps & pads. See Ad pg 55.

Goldline Percussion Products 208.265.5353

Grover Pro Percussion 617.935.6200

King Kong Kases 800.776.1525

Protune Corp. 914.462.6542

Vaughncraft Percussion 913.255.4500

CASES & COVERS

Any Gig Products 615.381.6854

King Kong Kases 800.776.1525

On the Case Productions 404.320.7546

Small Dog Products
574 Boston Avenue, Medford MA 02155
P: 617.396.0662 **F:** 617.396.0712
Timpani travel bag, 4 grab handles, top zipper,
pocket, extra padded bottom, any size, waterproof nylon w/ man-made shearling lining. Call for
free catalog. **See Coupon Section for $avings.**

CYMBALS

Meinl (USA) 804.560.4840

Paiste America 800.472.4783

Sabian, Ltd. 506 272 2019

CONCERT

UFIP Earcrafted Cymbals
101 Bernoulli Circle,93030
P: 805 485.6999 **F:**805 485.1334
UFIP Class, Experience, Natural & Rough cymbals are "earcreated" by Italian artisans for a unique yet musical sound & performance.

Zildjian Cymbal Co. 617.871.2200

DAMPENERS & MUFFLERS

Husher Int'l, Ltd.
PO Box 71, Sayville NY 11782
P: 516.471.7275
Husher's design allows "real feel" response, bounce & tone with 90% less volume. Even brushes can be used. Be smart, Practice safe sound!
See ad pg. 9 **& Coupon Section for $avings.**

DRUMS

Ajax - Netherlands 31.20.6596858

Black Swamp Percussion
13493 New Holland St., Holland MI 49424
P: 616.738.3190 **F:** 616.738.3105
Eml: info@blackswampcom
Drums, 8",10", & 12 tambourines, castanets, triangles, snare systems, world class instruments played by top professionals.

The Clevelander Drum Co. 216.691.9152

Grover Pro Percussion 617.935.6200

Ludwig Industries 219.522.1675

Orpheus Music 800.821.9448

Stingray Percussion 561.848.4489

Striker Drum Co. 610.296.5554

The Clevelander Drum Co. 216.691.9152

Vancore Timpani- Netherlands . . .31.513.415127

Yamaha Corp. of America 616.940.4900

CONCERT

HARDWARE

Goldline Percussion Products 208.265.5353

Grover Music Products 800.321.0556

Hyer Percussion 888.Hyer.Per

Stotz Cable Timpani 716.436.7630

XL Specialty Percussion Inc.
6335-5 Lima Road, Huntertown IN 46748
P: 800.348.1012 **F:** 219.637.6354
Eml: xlspl@aol.com
XL suspended Bass drum stand- strong unique
design offers easy, quiet positioning for 32", 36',
40" bass drum. Call for free Catalog.

HEADS

Grover Pro Percussion 617.935.6200

Striker Drum Co. 610.296.5554

United Rawhide 773.276.1177

KEYBOARD PERCUSSION

Demorrow Instruments Ltd. 501.246.4010

Fall Creek Marimbas 716.554.4011

Hyer Percussion 888.Hyer.Per

Kori Percussion 810.546.4135

Ludwig Industries 219.522.1675

Malletech 908.774.0088

Marimba One
PO Box 786, Arcata CA 95518
P: 707.822.9570/ 888.990.6663 **F:** 707.822.6256
Marimba One custom manufactures the finest
quality marimbas in today's market.

Orpheus Music 800.821.9448

Ross Mallet Instruments 512.288.7400

Yamaha Corp. of America 616.940.4900

GAMBAL MALLETS

KEYBOARD MALLETS

CONCERT BASS MALLETS

GONG MALLETS

BRUSHES

DRUM KEYS

TOM MALLETS

BASS MALLETS

CYMBAL STRAPS & PADS

P.O. Box 452, Chinchilla, PA 18420
Tel: (717) 457-8903 • Fax: (717) 457-8906
E-Mail: gambalmlts@aol.com

CONCERT

MALLET & STICKS

A.B.C. Percussion Mallets- UK . . .31.78.6173845

Century Mallet Instruments 312.248.7733

Cooperman Fife & Drum Co.: 860.767.1779

Dave Morby Timpani Sticks- UK . . .44.1284.830500

Encore Mallets, Inc.
702 Runge Dr., Lewisville TX 75057
P: 972.436.6963 **F:** 972.436.6963
"Marimba, xylo, vibe, bell, latex, timpani, marching
mallets w/ rattan, birch & fiberglass shafts. Call for
free catalog. **See Coupon Section of $avings.**

Equilibrium 313.426.5814

Gambal Mfg.
PO Box 452, Chinchilla PA 18410-0452
P: 717.457.8903 **F:** 717.457.8906
Eml: gambalmlts@aol.com
Mallets for keyboard, concert bass & gongs,
toms & bass. Brushes, drum keys, cymbal
straps & pads. See Ad pg 55.

Hyer Percussion 888.Hyer.Per

Inaki Sebastion Mallets 0034.43.33.12.41

JC's Drum Shop 410.661.7507

Jopo Music / Diamond Tip 818.995.6208

Ludwig Industries 219.522.1675

Malletech 908.774.0088

Mano a Mano Symphonic Mallets . . 972.613.2235

Mike Balter Mallets 847.541.5777

The Clevelander Drum Co. 216.691.9152

Percussion Construction
PO Box 6116, Kingwood T3X 77325
P: 800.3.mallet **F:** 713.360.4104
Percussion Construction offers a full line of eco-
nomically priced keyboard mallets.

Pro-Mark Corp. 800.822.1492

Regal Tip (Calato Mfg) 800.358.4590

The Clevelander Drum Co. 216.691.9152

Vic Firth, Inc. 617.326.3455

MARCHING

ACCESSORIES

Cooperman Fife & Drums 860.767.1779

Drum Corp Dale's 412.224.6307

CASES

King Kong Kases 800.776.1525

On the Case Prod. 800.Case.102

XL Specialty Percussion Inc. 800.348.1012

CYMBALS

Meinl (USA) 804.560.4840

Paiste America 800.472.4783

Sabian, Ltd. 506.272.2019

Zildjian Cymbal Co. 617.871.2200

DAMPENERS & MUFFLERS

Husher Int'l, Ltd.
PO Box 71 Sayville NY 11782
P: 516.471.7275
Husher's design allows "real feel" response, bounce &
tone with 90% less volume. Even brushes can be
used. Be smart, Practice safe sound! See ad pg. 14 **&
Coupon Section for $avings.**

DRUMS

Cooperman Fife & Drum Co. 860.767.1779

DEG Music Products, Inc. 414.248.8314

Impact Industries 715.842.1651

Ludwig Industries 219.522.1675

Monolith Composite 905.689.6173

Pearl Corp 615.833.4477

MARCHING

DRUMS cont'd

REMO, Inc.
28101 Industry Drive, Valencia CA 91355
P: 805.294.5630/ 800.525.5134 **F:** 805.294.5700
Web: www.remousa.com
Remo's commitment to marching perc. includes a full
range of hi-tension marching drumheads as well as
corp-tested marching snares, multi-toms & bass drums.

Stingray Percussion 561.848.4489

The Clevelander Drum Co. 216.691.9152

Yamaha Corp. of America 616.940.4900

HARDWARE

LP Music
160 Belmont Ave., Garfield NJ 07026
P: 973 478.6903 **F:** 973 772.3568
Web: lpmusic.com
Percussion marching carrier. Call for more info.

Pearl Corp 615.833.4477

XL Specialty Percussion Inc. 800.348.1012

MIDI CONTROLLERS

Walkabout Inc.
3985 Meier St.,Los Angeles CA 90066
P: 310.306.2701/ 800.430.Walk **F:** 310.306.3732
Eml: go4walk@aol.com

MARCHING

PRACTICE ACCESSORIES

Drum Corp Dale's
528 W. 9th Ave., Tarentum PA 15084
P: 412.224.6307 **F:** 412.226.3232
Woodshed: Practice goal: Direction full size quint set/ table top & lap top practice pads. To help you get where you are willing to go!

Xymox 909.390.6995

STICKS & MALLET

Aquarian Accessories Corp 800.473.0231

Cooperman Fife & Drum Co.: 860.767.1779

Encore Mallets, Inc.
702 Runge Dr., Lewisville TX 75057
P: 972.436.6963 **F:** 972.436.6963
Marimba, xylo, vibe, bell, latex, timpani, marching mallets w/ rattan, birch & fiberglass shafts. Call for free catalog. **See Coupon Section for $avings.**

Impact Industries 715.842.1651

Innovative Percussion 615.333.9388

JC's Drum Shop 410.661.7507

Percussion Construction
PO Box 6116, Kingwood TX 77325
P: 800.3.mallet **F:** 713.360.4104
Percussion Construction offers a full line of economically priced keyboard mallets. Catalog n/c.
See Coupon Section for $avings.

Pro-Mark Corp. 800.822.1492

Regal Tip (Calato Mfg) 800.358.4590

WEARABLES

Rhythm Wear
PO Box 1238, Arlington VA 02174
P/F: 617.776.7206
Award-winning music related & custom t-shirt designs, featuring in-your-face & field drumming themes. Custom made bomber leather sleeve tour jackets. Screenprinting, embroidery, design. Wholesale, fundraising & namedrop.

ELECTRONICS

ACCESSORIES

Ac-cetera, Inc 800.537.3491

Garwood Communications 215.860.6866

HQ Percussion Products 800.467.3335

Mackie Designs 206.487.4333

DRUM KITS

A.D. Speaker Systems 803.626.3415

A.P. Boom Theory 206.850.8656

Dauz Drum Co. 818.758.9272

ddrum/ Armadillo Enterprises 800.793.5273

Drum Tech 413.538.7586

Electronic Perc. Systems/GMDI 770.300.0707

Hart Dynamnics Inc. 800.769.5335

K & K Sound Systems
935 S. Empire Blvd.. Coos Bay OR 97420
P: 541.888.3517/ 800.To.Sound **F:** 541.888.4846
Electronic Drum Kits -Professional trigger equipment and pads.

Korg USA 516.333.9100

Roland Corp./ Musical Instruments 213.685.5141

S&S Industries / GMDI 770.300.0707

Simmons Services 818.887.6708

Yamaha Corp. of America 616.940.4900

DRUM MACHINES

Alesis Corp. 310.558.4530

Boss / Roland Corp 213.685.5141

ELECTRONICS

HEADPHONES

GK Music	800.747.5545
Metrophones / Big Bang Distribution	818.727.1127
Sennheiser	860.434.9190
Shure	800.25.Shure

METRONOMES

Innovations FM7 Inc.	418.856.3387
Interactive Metronome	616.975.1245
Russian Dragon	800.880.8776

MICROPHONES

ELECTRONICS

MICROPHONES cont'd

AKG Acoustics 800.878.7571

Applied Microphone Technologies 201.992.7699

Audix 800.966.8261

Beyer Dynamic 516.293.3200

Calac / Big Bang Distribution 818.727.1127

Donnell Enterprises 800.585.7659

Earthworks 603.654.2423

Electro Voice 800.234.6831

K & K Sound Systems
935 S. Empire Blvd., Coos Bay OR 97420
P: 541.888.3517/ 800.To.Sound **F:** 541.888.4846
High Quality Microphones for drums and percussion.

Nady Systems 510.652.2411

Pan Electric 403.285.8893

Peavey Electronics Corp. 601.483.5365

Randall May International 714.757.1717

SHURE
222 Hartrey Avenue, Evanston IL 60202
P: 847.866.2200/ 800.25.Shure **F:** 847.866.2279
Manufacturer of premium-quality drum mics. Call for free catalog & "Mic techniques for live sound reinforcement" booklet. See ad pg 63.

MIDI CONTROLLER

Walkabout Inc.
PO Box 66058 St.,Los Angeles CA 90066
P: 310.306.2701/ 800.430.Walk **F:**310.306.3732
Eml: go4walk@aol.com
Mobile midi systems for percussion & keyboard controllers. Battery powered & wireless, for live performance. Catalog n/c. See Ad pg 59.

ELECTRONICS

SAMPLE SOURCES

Drumtrax 508.977.0570

Sampleheads, Inc. 212.262.3488

TRIGGERS

Concept 1 Percussion 800.822.9602

ddrum/ Armadillo Enterprises 800.793.5273

Drum Tech 413.538.7586

Electronic Perc. Systems/ GMDI . . 770.300.0707

Fishman Transducers, Inc. 800.fishman

Hart Dynamnics Inc. 800.769.5335

K & K Sound Systems
935 S. Empire Blvd., Coos Bay OR 97420
P: 541.888.3517/ 800.To.Sound **F:** 541.888.4846
Triggers - Unique amplification and midi systems for mallet instruments.

KAT / Emu Systems 408.438.1921

Layon Drum Triggers 801.967.4135

Mystique Sound Solutions 612.488.1560

Pintech Inc. 864.609.5735

S&S Industries / GMDI 770.300.0707

Softapads- England 44.113.286.5381

Technical Knock Out!
PO Box 92377, Nashville TN 37209-8377
P: 615.292.1929 **F:** 615.386.9979
Technical Knock Out Drum Triggers. Guarantee - Audio/ Inst. Cables- $ave! Free Catalog.
See Coupon Section for $avings.

Trigger Perfect / GMDI 770.300.0707

Zendrum Corp. 404.352.1646

XL 100% Cotton T's • Only $15

Specify Style A (Blk or Wht Shirt) or Style B (Blk only)

Please add $5 for S/H • NY State residents add $8\frac{1}{4}$ sales tax

RETAIL

USED/VINTAGE

INT'L RETAIL

RENTAL

CARTAGE

REPAIR SVCS

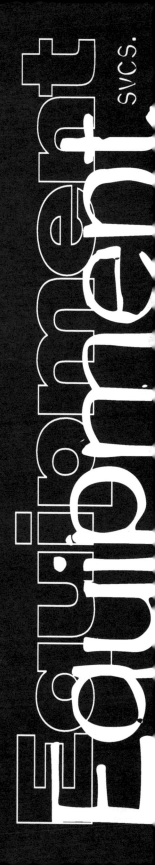

Equipment Svcs.

R E T A I L

ALABAMA

Area Code 205

Art's Music Shop	Montgomery	800.341.2787
Bailey Bros. Music	Montgomery	205.262.7827
Birmingham Perc. Ctr	Birmingham	205.823.9911
Crossroad Music	Auburn	205.887.7735
Decade Music	Tuscaloosa	205.750.0095
Emiron	Decatur	205.353.0772
Gadsden Music	Gadsden	800.264.7228
Galaxy Music	Florence	205.767.0009
Major Music	Decatur	205.353.5633
Nuncie's Music	Birmingham	205.252.4498
Pro Music	Decatur	205.350.8533

Area Code 334

Andy's Music	Mobile	334.633.8944
Metro Music	Dothan	334.792.0883
MMI Music	Mobile	334.660.1277
Strickland Music	Dothan	334.792.7197

ALASKA

Area Code 907

Mamoth Musical	Anchorage	907.272.9944
McPherson Music	Ketchikan	800.478.3650
Music Works	Anchorage	907.562.5481

ARIZONA

Area Code 520

Chicago Stores	Tucson	520.622.3341

ARIZONA cont'd

De-No Music Ctr.	Casa Grande	520.836.2601
Guitars etc.	Tucson	520.748.1111
Prescott Music Ctr.	Prescott	520.445.5030
Rainbow Guitars	Tucson	520.325.3376
Sticks n' Strings	Tucson	520.296.3479
The Drum Shop	Prescott	520.771.0216
Westside Music	Tucson	520.578.2427

Area Code 602

All Star Music	Mesa	602.832.8800
Birdland	Yuma	602.344.8643
Bizarre Guitar & Drums	Phoenix	602.248.9297
Boogie Music City	Phoenix	602.978.6688
Brengle's Music	Mesa	602.892.0681
Brindley Music	Chandler	602.963.1468
Buchanan Music	Mesa	602.461.9161
Castaneda's Music	Phoenix	602.849.0608
Cedar Music Inc	Flagstaff	602.779.0799
Central Music	Phoenix	602.274.6307
D.J.'s Music	Phoenix	602.275.0654
Dave's Drum Shop	Scottsdale	602.951.3451
De Bell Music	Yuma	602.782.3937
Dog House Music Ctr.	Avondale	602.925.1082
Flagstaff Music Ctr.	Flagstaff	602.774.4321
Forte' Music	Phoenix	602.548.1114
Guitar Ctr.	Tempe	602.753.6900
Guitar Ctr.	Phoenix	602.375.3800
Milano Music	Mesa	602.834.6581
Milano Music	Scottsdale	602.443.1703
Sound City Music	Tempe	602.921.2702

R E T A I L

ARKANSAS

Area Code 501

Ace Music	Fayetteville	501.636.0229
Applings Music	Hot Springs	501.623.1212
Back Beat Music	Jonesboro	501.932.7529
Bensbergs Music	Camden	501.836.6844
Boyd's Music Ctr	Little Rock	501.664.3614
Center Stage Music	Little Rock	501.225.6962
Charleston Music	Charleston	501.965.2332
Musician's Pro Shop	Springdale	501.756.8742
Romco Drums	Little Rock	501.666.0814
Ronnie's Steel Guitar	Hot Springs	501.623.4603
Stonehenge Music	Little Rock	501.568.2380
Texarkana Pro	Texarkana	501.774.2003

CALIFORNIA

Area Code 209

Bentley's Drum Shop	Fresno	209.222.5011
Miracle Music	Stockton	209.466.4388
Skip's Music	Modesto	209.522.1003
Soundstage Music	Fresno	209.233.6531
Spitzer Music Pro Drum	Stockton	209.466.4388
Spitzer Music Pro Drum	Fresno	209.233.6531

Area Code 213

City Of Drums	Hollywood	213.465.4524
Guitar Ctr.	Hollywood	213.874.1060
Pro Drum Shop	Hollywood	213.469.6285

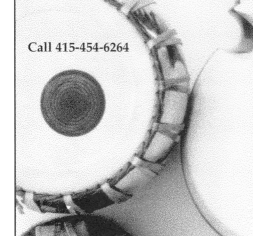

R E T A I L

CALIFORNIA cont'd

Area Code 310

Downey Music	Downey	310.869.4485
Guitar Ctr.	Lawndale	310.542.9444
Guitar Ctr.	South Bay	310.542.9444
Noisy Toys	Westchester	310.670.9957
Rockit Music	Whittier	310.902.9227
W. LA Music Drum Ctr.	W. LA	310.477.1945

Area Code 408

Drum Bwhana	Aptos	408.685.6135
Guitar Ctr.	San Jose	408.249.0455
Music Unlimited	Monterey	408.372.5893
Rhythm Fusion	Santa Cruz	408.423.2048 *831.423-*
Starving Musician	Santa Clara	408.554.9041
Union Grove Music	Santa Cruz	408.427.0670

Area Code 415

A Drummer's Tradition	San Rafael	415.458.1688

Ali Akbar College
215 W. End Ave. San Rafael, CA 94901
P: 800.74.Tabla **Eml:** aacm@ix.netcom.com
Web: http://pomo.nbn.com/home/aacm/
Finest Instruments from India. See ad pg 71.

Drum World	San Francisco	415.334.7559
Gelb Music	Redwood City	415.365.8878
Guitar Ctr.	San Francisco	415.626.7655
Haight Ashbury	San Francisco	415.863.7327
Magic Flute	San Rafael	415.479.3112
Sam Adato's Drum	San Francisco	415.863.3786

Area Code 510

Allegro Music	Fremont	510.793.3500
D'Amico Drums	Fremont	510.226.8700

CALIFORNIA cont'd

Guitar Ctr.	East Bay	510.559.1055
Guitar Ctr.	Pleasant Hill	510.825.8880
Spitzer Pro Drum	Concord	510.676.3151

Area Code 562

Whittaker Music	Long Beach	562.598.2461

Area Code 619

Gary's Drum Studio	Apple Valley	619.242.8772
Guitar Ctr.	San Diego	619.583.9751
Music Mart	San Diego	619.695.8144
New World Music & Sound	San Diego	619.569.1944
San Diego Drum & Perc.	Vista	619.945.3935

Area Code 707

Gordon's Music & Sound	Fairfield	707.422.0313
Lark in the Morning	Mendocino	707.964.5569
Petaluma Music Ctr	Petaluma	707.778.7171
Rhythm Matters	Santa Rosa	707.523.Drum
Zone Music	Cotati	707.664.1213

Area Code 714

Guitar Ctr.	Brea	714.672.0103
Guitar Ctr.	Fountain Valley	714.241.9140
Huntington Music	Huntington Bch	714.848.9280
Mission Music	Mission Viejo	714.347.0900
Music to the Max	Westminster	714.379.1994
Orange Cnty Drum & Perc	R.S.M.	714.589.7308
West Coast Drum Ctr.	Santa Ana	714.545.2345

Area Code 760

Guitar Ctr.	San Marcos	760.735.8050

CALIFORNIA cont'd

Area Code 805

American Music Ctr.	Oxnard	805.485.1181
Mike's Drum Shop	Santa Barbara	805.962.1211
The Drum Circuit	San Luis Obispo	805.543.0338
Valley Drum Shop	Thousand Oaks	805.497.9055
Wally World Music	Thousand Oaks	805.496.8322
World Music	Simi Valley	805.526.9351

Area Code 818

Big Valley Music	Northridge	818.772.1668
Charles Music	Glendale	818.242.6597
Drum Doctors	N. Hollywood	818.506.8123
Drum Paradise	N. Hollywood	818.762.7878
Guitar Ctr.	Sherman Oaks	818.990.8332
Guitar Ctr.	Covina	818.967.7911
Hermes Music	Sherman Oaks	818.986.3260

Area Code 909

Alta Loma Music	Rcho. Cucamonga	909.989.5757
Guitar Ctr.	San Bernadino	909.383.3700
K.J. Music	Alta Loma	909.989.0246

Ontario Music
215 W. "G" St. Ontario, CA 91762
P: 909.983.3551 **F:** 909.988.2272
Hrs: M-Th: 10 - 8, Fri & Sat: 10 - 6
Venues served: All southern California w/same day svc avail. **Svcs:** Ship anywhere,Fed Ex, UPS .
Brand lines: Ludwig, Tama, Pearl, Premier, DW, Sabian, Zildjian, Paiste, LP, Toca.

Area Code 916

Cameron Park Music		916.676.5422
Drum & Guitar City	Sacramento	916.383.2489
Northridge Music Ctr	Citrus Hts	916.969.4728
Skip's Music	Sacramento	916.484.7575

RETAIL

COLORADO

Area Code 303

Brentwood Music . . . . . . .Denver   303.935.2101

Drum City-Guitarland, Inc.
9225 W. 44th Ave., Wheat Ridge CO 80033
P: 303.421.4515 .**F:** 303.421.1155
Eml: dcgl@ix.netcom.com
Hrs: M-F 11-6PM Sat. 11-5 Closed Sunday
Venues served: Red-Rocks, Fiddler's Green,
Mammoth Events Ctr., Bluebird, Ogden Theatres,
McNichols. Same day delivery avl. **Svcs:** Ship any-
where via Fedex, UPS. **Brand lines:** Discount prices
since 1965. DW, Pearl, Yamaha, Tama, Sonor, Ludwig,
Nbl & Cooley, Zildjian, Paiste, Sabian.

Evergreen Music . . . . .Evergreen   303.674.2371

Fred's Music Ctr. . . . .Englewood   303.788.0707

Overseas Connection . .Broomfield   800.766.6048

Pro Sound . . . . .Boulder   303.530.1364

Rockley Music . . . . . . .Lakewood   303.233.4444

Rupp's Drums
2160 S. Holly St. Denver, CO 80222
P: 303.756.5777 **F:** 303.757.2792
Hrs. M-F: 10.- 7, S: 10 - 6, Sun: 12 - 5
Venues served: McNichols Arena, Red-Rocks,
Fiddler's Green, Mammoth Evans Ctr, Bluebird
& Ogden Theatres w/same day svc avail.
Svcs: Ship anywhere, Fed Ex, Airborne, UPS.
Brand lines: DW, Tama, Premier, Sonor, Legend,
Remo, all percussion lines, all cymbals.

Area Code 719

Colorado Springs Music
Colorado Springs 719.635.1561

Rice Music Inc. .Colorado Springs   719.634.3717

Area Code 970

Colorado Drum & Perc.
Fort Collins 970.229.9473

Glenwood Music
Glenwood Springs 970.928.8628

Planetary Perc. . . . . .Aspen   970.920.2124

equip.

75

svcs.

R E T A I L

CONNECTICUT

Area Code 203

Beller's Music	Manchester	203.649.2036
Burritt Music	New Britain	203.229.2069
Caruso's Music	New London	203.442.9600
Charlie Donnely's Drum	Newington	203.667.0535
Connecticut Music	Stamford	203.348.1857
Cos Cob Music	Cos Cob	203.869.2432
D'Addario Music	Stratford	203.377.1315
Daddy's Junkie Music	Orange	203.799.3239
Daddy's Junkie Music	Stamford	203.975.8020
Fladd Music	Milford	203.874.3497
Goldie & Libro Music	New Haven	203.562.5133
Gordon-La Salle Music	East Hartford	203.289.3500
Greenwich Music	Greenwich	203.869.3615
James Daniels Music	Stamford	203.324.6667
Music Plus	Danbury	203.744.4344
Norwalk Music	Norwalk	203.847.3925
Ron's Guitars	Groton Ct.	203.445.0194
Sam Ash Music	New Haven	203.389.0500

Area Code 860

Creative Music	Wethersfield	860.563.1098
Daddy's Junkie Music	Hartford	860.224.4648
Daddy's Junkie Music	Vernon	860.644.5342
The Music Shop	Avon	860.676.1311

R E T A I L

D.C.

Area Code 202

Percussion 'N Things
633 Allison At. NW, Washington DC 20011
P: 202.291.6577 / 9397 **F:** 202.882.4649
Hrs: M-Sat.: 11-7, Sun: Closed
Venues served: Kennedy Ctr, Constitution Hall, Nat'l
Thtr, Warner Thtr, WolfTrax, MCI Ctr, Merryweather
Post Pav., Carter Baron Amph. w/same day svc avail.
Svcs: Ship anywhere UPS. **Brand lines:** Authentic
African djembe's & balafons (incl. childrens models),
djun-djuns, sangba's, bells, koras, e'goni's, log drums
(krins), talking drums (tamas), African castanets,
gourd shekeres, Lalas, hairless goatskins, & ltd.
selection of drums from Ghana.

DELAWARE

Area Code 302

Concord Music	Newark	302.454.7664
Drum Pad Music	Felton	302.284.4664
First Call Music	Newark	302.366.8750
G & G Music Inc.	Wilmington	302.478.5188
Michael G's Music	Wilmington	302.475.9320
Mid-Atlantic Music	Wilmington	302.995.7170

R E T A I L

FLORIDA

Area Code 305

Abe Music	Miami	305.220.1927
Abe Music	N. Miami	305.944.7429
Ace Music	Miami	305.891.6201
Allegro Music	Miami	305.442.8948
Guitar Ctr.	Kendall	305.271.2600
Guitar Ctr.	Miami	305.271.2600
Music Arts Ent.	Ft. Lauderdale	305.581.2203
Resurrection Drums	Miami	305.559.6719
Sam Ash	Miami Lakes	305.628.3510

Area Code 352

Band Central Station	Gainesville	352.371.9057
Music & Stuff	Mount Dora	352.735.5505
Scott Tennyson's	Gainsville	352.371.2571
Sound Exchange	Ocala	352.694.7290

Area Code 407

Ace Music	Orlando	407.629.2288
Discount Music Ctr.	Orlando	407.423.4171
Florida Discount Music	Melbourne	407.254.5645
Florida Music Svc	Tampa	800.229.8863
George's Music	Orlando	407.352.8000
Jammer Dscnt Music	Kissimmee	407.847.6744
Music Mart	Orlando	407.273.2010
Thoroughbred Music	Orlando	407.599.1222

Area Code 561

Academy of Music	Ft. Pierce	561.464.3533
Drum World	W. Palm Beach	561.471.8266
Schumacher Music	Stuart	561.286.7474

RETAIL

FLORIDA cont'd

Area Code 813

Bringe Music	St. Petersburg	813.822.3460
Express Music	Seminole	813.392.5922
Key of Sea Music	Clearwater	813.787.8822
Paragon Music Ctr	Tampa	813.876.3459
Thoroughbred Music	Clearwater	813.725.8062
Thoroughbred Music	Tampa	813.889.3874
Thoroughbred Music	Sarasota	813.351.7793

Area Code 904

Brass & Reed Music	Daytona Bch	904.252.5544
Discount Music Ctr.	Jacksonville	904.387.6527
Harris Music & Sound	Pensacola	904.434.6497
Leitz Music	Panama City	904.769.0111
Music Xchange	Tallahassee	904.224.2662
Pro Music	Jacksonville	904.399.5719
Scott Tennyson's	Tallahassee	904.222.9660

Area Code 954

Ace Music	Ft. Lauderdale	954.733.8400
Guitar Ctr.	Hallandale	954.456.7890
Resurrection Drums	Hallandale	954.457.9020

GEORGIA

Area Code 404

Atlanta Drums & Perc.	Atlanta	800.598.5177
Attina's Music	Forrest Park	404.361.7932
Dekalb Musicians Supply Decatur		404.378.3100
Guitar Ctr.	Atlanta	404.320.7253

GEORGIA cont'd

Area Code 404 cont'd

Pepper of Atlanta	Atlanta	800.345.6296
Symmes Music	Atlanta	800.966.4027

Area Code 706

A World of Music	Augusta	706.650.9977
Colaianni Music	Columbus	706.323.1809
Columbus Music	Columbus	706.569.5004
Jay's Music & Sound	Augusta	706.736.1250

Area Code 770

Atlanta Discount Music	Atlanta	770.457.3400
Atlanta Pro Perc.	Smyrna	770.Ido.Drum
Attina's Music Stores	Fayetteville	770.461.2699
Dirt Cheep Music	Smyrna	770.433.0196
Great Southern Perc.	Cartersville	770.606.9009
Guitar Ctr.	Smyrna	770.433.2777
Ken Stanton Music	Marietta	770.427.2491
Ken Stanton Music	Roswell	770.993.8334
Keynote Music	Conyers	770.483.9508
Music & Arts Ctr.	Alpharetta	770.993.4428
Music & Arts Ctr.	Marietta	770.977.7073
Pro Music	Gainesville	770.535.2370
Pro Music	Gainesville	770.535.2370

Area Code 912

Bibb Music Ctr.	Macon	912.746.3232
Bill Hardin Music	Macon	912.781.1112
Carl Corbin Music	Macon	912.788.6700
Clyde's Discount Music Brunswick		912.261.8650
Portman Music	Savannah	912.354.1500

equip.
80
svcs.

RETAIL

HAWAII

Area Code 808

Bounty Music	Kahului	808.871.1141
Drummers Warehouse	Honolulu	808.942.7000
Fred Vinson's Drums	Honolulu	808.533.7550
Free Spirits	Honomu	808.963.6121
Harry's Music Store	Honolulu	808.735.2866

IDAHO

Area Code 208

American Music	Caldwell	208.454.0330
Burt's Music	Coeur D'Alene	208.664.4957
Chesbro Music Co.	Idaho Falls	208.522.8691
Dorsey Music	Nampa	208.466.5681
Dorsey Music	Boise	208.853.4141
Greif's Music	Payette	208.642.9033
Music Ctr.	Twin Falls	208.733.8609

ILLINOIS

Area Code 217

Big Dawg Music	Quincy	217.228.3294
Dave's Music Co.	Rantoul	217.893.3817
Skins & Tins Drums	Champaign	217.352.3786
Z's Music	Charleston	217.345.2616

Area Code 309

Don's Music Land	Peoria	309.692.0854
Elmore Music Warehouse	Peoria	309.692.1253
Pro Sound Ctr.	Normal	309.888.4500

equip.
81
svcs.

RETAIL

ILLINOIS cont'd

Area Code 312

Chicago Perc. Ctr. . . . . .Chicago   312.341.0102

Area Code 618

Cowabunga Music . . . . . . .Anna   618.833.3903

Fornaszewski Drum Shop
Granite City 618.877.3475

Marching Music Ltd. . . .Belleville   618.394.9665

Miller Music . . . . . . .Fairview Hts   618.277.2002

Swing City . . . . .Collinsville   618.345.6700

Area Code 630

Brookdale Music . . . . .Naperville   630.983.5100

Guitar Ctr. . . . . .Villa Park   630.832.2800

Area Code 708

Drum Ctr. . . . . .Wheeling   708.459.1255

Gand Music & Sound . .Northfield   708.446.4263

Guitar Ctr. . . . . .Burbank   708.422.1400

Midwest Perc. . . .Chicago Ridge   708.499.2314

Roselle Music . . . . .Roselle   708.529.2031

Area Code 773

Biasco Music . . . . .Chicago   773.286.5900

Flatts & Sharpe Music . .Chicago   773.465.5233

Guitar Ctr. . . . . .Chicago   773.327.5687

Musicians Network . . . .Chicago   773.728.2929

Snukst . . . . .Chicago   773.585.7923

Area Code 815

Guzzardo Music . . . . . .Rockford   815.229.5020

Area Code 847

Guitar Ctr. . . . . . . .Arlington Hts   847.439.4600

Karnes Music . . . . . .Des Plaines   847.298.1335

R E T A I L

Karnes Music . . . . .Schaumburg   847.517.7756

Karnes Music . . . . . .Vernon Hills   847.367.1681

The Drum Pad
48 W. Palatine Rd. Palatine, IL 60067
P: 847.934.8768 **F:** 847.934.8797
Hrs: M-Th: 12 - 9, F: 12 - 6, S: 11 - 4, Sun. 12 -4
Venues served: Rosemont Horizon, Rosemont
Thtr w/same day svc avail. **Svcs:** Mail order, UPS.
Brand lines: Pearl, Tama, Yamaha, Ludwig, Premier,
GMS, Legend, Trick, DW, Sonor, Roland, Ayotte.

Total Music . . . . .Glenview   847.724.5310

INDIANA

Area Code 219

Broadway Music . . . . . .Crown Pt.   219.736.7706

Decatur Music House . . .Decatur   219.724.3353

Drums in the Wind . . .South Bend   219.272.8266

Paxton Music . . . . .Valparaiso   219.462.5086

Tri State Music . . . . . .Fort Wayne   219.483.1007

Area Code 317

Drum Ctr. of Indianapolis 317.594.8989

Family Music Ctr. . . .Indianapolis   317.542.0183

Indie Drum Connection
Indianapolis 317 293.5057

IRC Music Stores . . .Indianapolis   317.849.7965

Paige's Music . . . . . .Indianapolis   800.345.6296

Area Code 812

Butler Music . . . . .Brazil   812.446.0852

Dallas Music . . . . .Evansville   812.423.1493

Far Out Music . . . . .Jeffersonville   812.282.1122

Music Shoppe . . . . . .Terre Haute   812.232.4095

R E T A I L

IOWA

Area Code 319

England Music Ctr . . . . . .Clinton   319.242.1604

Griggs Music Inc. . . . .Davenport   319.391.9000

Sixteenth Ave. Music
Cedar Rapids 319.362.1987

Area Code 515

Boyer Music . . . . .Mason City   515.423.7785

Fort Dodge Music . . .Fort Dodge   515.576.6160

Ground Zero Music . . . .Indianola   515.961.8917

Professional Music . .Des Moines   515.243.7648

Area Code 712

Flood Music . . . . .Sioux City   712.255.5412

KANSAS

Area Code 316

Belli Brothers Music Svcs.
McPherson 316.241.5557

Brier & Hale Music . . . . . .Liberal   316.624.8421

C Major Guitars . . . . .Wichita   316.682.8182

Flemming Music . . . . . . .Chanute   316.431.1272

Garrison Music . . . . .Emporia   316.342.4553

Midwest Drum & Perc. . . .Wichita   316.265.3070

Area Code 785

C & C Drum Shop . . . . . .Topeka   785.235.3786

Area Code 913

Funk's Music Ctr. . . . . .Olathe   913.764.4158

Glenn's Music . . . . . . .Manhattan   913.539.1926

Harmonic Arts . . . . . . .Lawrence   913.842.3321

Top Cat Perc. . . . . . .Kansas City   913.782.2174

RETAIL

KENTUCKY

Area Code 502

Mom's Music . . . . .Louisville   502.899.3344

Music Warehouse . . . . .Louisville   502.456.4730

3rd Planet Music . . . . .Louisville   502.423.0001

Unga Bunga Music . . . .Paducah   502.441.9000

Area Code 606

Carl's Music Ctr. . . . . . .Lexington   606.254.0324

Currier's Music World . .Richmond   606.623.6010

Don Wilson Music . . . .Lexington   606.278.7459

Drum Ctr. of Lexington .Lexington   606.276.1827

Maschinot Music . . . . . .Newport   606.491.1552

Pied Piper Music . . . . . .Ashland   606.325.7664

LOUISIANA

Area Code 318

Cenla Music . . . . .Alexandria   318.443.9010

Enchanted Forest . . .Lake Charles   318.433.7737

Matt's Music . . . . .Monroe   318.387.3628

Vince's Backstage . . . . .Lafayette   318.999.1717

Zeagler Music . . . . .Monroe   318.322.2621

Area Code 504

Bonnee Band Shop .Morgan City   504.384.1832

Chalmette Music Co. . .Chalmette   504.277.0440

Drum Shop . . . . .Gretna   504.362.9538

Fabregas Music Store . . .Houma   504.873.7461

Fransen's Drum Ctr. . . . .Kenner   504.466.8484

Michael Noto's Music Baton Rouge   504.272.2782

Zeagler Music . . . . .Baton Rouge   504.933.0769

equip.
85
svcs.

RETAIL

MAINE

Area Code 207

Al Corey's Music Ctr. . . .Waterville	207.872.5622
Carroll's Music Ctr. . . . . .Lewiston	207.782.2545
Down Home Music . . . . .Fairfield	207.453.2942
Drum Shop . . . . .Portland	207 874.6630
Ezzy's Music Shop . . . .Van Buren	207.868.2838
Portland Perc. . . . . .Portland	207.775.2230

MARYLAND

Area Code 301

Drums on Sale . . . . .Hagerstown	301.733.Drum
Drums Unlimited Inc. . .Bethesda	301.942.1332
Machen Music . . . . .Hagerstown	301.733.1441
Music & Arts Ctr. . . . . . . .Bowie	301.262.5950
Music & Arts Ctr. . . . . .Frederick	301.694.0007
Music & Arts Ctr. . . .Germantown	301.353.1113
Veneman Music . . . . . . .Rockville	301.231.6100
Washington Music . . . . .Wheaton	301.946.8808

Area Code 410

Baltimore Drum Source .Baltimore	410.661.1918
Baltimore Perc. Ctr. . . . .Baltimore	410.668.8677
Gordon Miller Music . . .Baltimore	410.825.2558
JC's Drum Shop . . . . . .Baltimore	410.661.7507
Master Musicians . . .Glen Burnie	410.766.7668
Music & Arts Ctr. . . . . . . .Bel Aire	410.569.3500
Music & Arts Ctr. . . .Cockeysville	410.667.9010
Music & Arts Ctr. . . . .Ellicott City	410.461.1844
Music & Arts Ctr. . . . . . .Rockville	410.544.1010

R E T A I L

MASSACHUSSETTS

Area Code 413

Downtown Sounds	.Northampton	413.586.0998
Falcetti Music Inc.	.Springfield	413.543.1002

Area Code 508

Centre Street Drums	.Brockton	508.559.5112
Daddy's Junkie Music	.Peabody	508.535.0123
Daddy's Junkie Music	.Shrewsbury	508.797.4421
Gordon-La Salle	.Southbridge	508.765.9352
Gordon-La Salle	.Worcester	508.753.8724
Guitar Center	.Danvers	508.777.1950
Guitar Center	.Natick	508.655.6525
Joe's Drum Shop	.Beverly	508.922.0200

Area Code 617

Cambridge Music Ctr.	.Cambridge	617.491.5433
Daddy's Junkie Music	.Boston	617.247.0909
Daddy's Junkie Music	.Dedham	617.329.9984
Daddy's Junkie Music	.Cambridge	617.497.1556
Dick Dicenso's Drum	.Quincy	617.479.1280
Guitar Ctr.	.Boston	617.738.5958
Matt's Music	.Hanover	617.829.0715

MICHIGAN

Area Code 313

Marshall Music Co.	Allen Park	313.383.5560
Pro Perc.	Plymouth	313.459.1212
RIT Music	Ann Arbor	313.930.1900
Trudell's Drum Shop	Garden City	313.425.3140
Wonderland Music	Dearborn	313.584.8111

Area Code 517

Elderly Instruments	Lansing	517.372.7880
Herter Music Ctr.	Bay City	517.893.4546
Music Manor	Lansing	517.393.5995
RIT Drums East	Saginaw	517.792.4777

Area Code 616

Dillon's Music World	Kalamazoo	616.344.5441
Farrow Music	Grand Rapids	616.538.8430
RIT Drums	Grand Rapids	616.243.7867
Sun Radius Music	Traverse City	616.922.9092

Area Code 810

Bill Schaffer's Drum Shop	Flushing	810.230.0620
Bogner Sound	Flint	810.238.8777
Guitar Ctr.	Detroit	810.296.6161
Herter Music Ctr.	Flint	810.732.7720
Huber-Breese Music	Fraser	810.294.3950
JC's Custom Drums	Rochester Hls	810.852.3660
Motor City Guitar	Waterford	810.683.2489
Music Villa	Livonia	810.477.0130
Pepper of Detroit	Troy	800.345.6296
Percussion World	Ferndale	810.543.7020
Sasko's Drum Shop	Center Line	810.759.1130
Southern Thumb Music	Richmond	810.727.2389
Wonderland Music	Bloomfield	810.855.6333

R E T A I L

MINNESOTA

Area Code 507

Eastman Music . . . . . . .Faribault   507.334.5434

Tone Music . . . . .Owatonna   507.451.5196

Tut's Drum Shack . . . . .Merrifield   800.770.9254

Area Code 612

B Sharp Music . . . . .Minneapolis   612.781.6838

Carlson Music Ctr. . . . .Alexandria   612.763.4011

Groth Music . . . . . . .Bloomington   800.969.4772

Guitar Ctr. . . . . .Roseville   612.631.9420

Schmitt Music . . . . . .Maplewood   612.770.0091

Schmitt Music . . . . .Edina   612.920.5080

Schmitt Music . . . . . .Minneapolis   612.339.3434

Schmitt Music . . . . . .Minnetonka   612.546.0555

Schmitt Music . . . . . . .Brookly Ctr   612.566.4560

Torps Music Ctr. . . . . . . .St. Paul   612.224.7621

MISSISSIPPI

Area Code 601

DC Music & Sound . . .Columbus   601.327.1555

Mississippi Music . . . . . .Jackson   601.922.1200

Mississippi Music . . . . . . .Biloxi   601.388.6547

Ronnie's Music Ctr. . . . . . .Pearl   601.939.5277

RETAIL

MISSOURI

Area Code 314

Drum Headquarters
7241 Manchester Rd. St. Louis, MO 63143
P: 314.644.0235 **F:** 314.644.4373
Eml: GtwyPerc@aol.com
Hrs: M-F: 11 - 8 , Sat: 10 - 5, Sun. Closed
Venues served: Kiel Center, Fox Thtr, Mississippi
Nights, Riverport w/same day svc avail. **Svcs:** mail
order, UPS. **Brand lines**: Every major line of drums
& percussion

Drum Headquarters
271 Centre Pointe Drive   St. Peters MO 63376
P: 314.8.0235 **F:** 314.928.2175
Hrs: M-F: 11 - 8 , Sat: 10 - 5, Sun. Closed
Venues served: Svcs: Brand lines: Same as
Above. Closer to Riverport.

Guitars & More	Arnold	314.296.6577

Area Code 417

Big Don's Music	Joplin	417.782.8505
Percussion Shop	Springfield	417.883.9112
Springfield Music	Springfield	417.881.1373

Area Code 573

Capital Music	Jefferson City	573.635.2732
Crazy Music Sound & Light Columbia		573.443.2559

Area Code 816

Antioch Music Ctr	Kansas City	816.455.2800
Big Dudes Music City	Kansas City	816.931.4638
C & C Drum Shop	Kansas City	816.468.1919
Explorer's Perc	Kansas City	816.361.1195
Gerhardt Music Svc	St. Joseph	816.232.0273
Kansas City Drum Works Kansas City		816.471.3786
Meyers Music	Blue Springs	816.228.5656
Quigly Music	Kansas City	816.361.2050

R E T A I L

MONTANA

Area Code 406

Bohemian Music	Billings	406.259.3610
Clark Music	Helena	406.442.1080
Dickinson Music	Missoula	406.549.0013
Drum Attic	Butte	406.723.4736
Electronic Sound & Perc.	Missoula	406.728.1117
Hansen Music	Billings	406.245.4544
Morgenroth Music Ctr.	Billings	406.723.4736
Rod's Music & Sound	Great Falls	406.771.1314

NEBRASKA

Area Code 308

Yanda's Music	Kearney	308.234.1970

Area Code 402

Dietz Music House	Lincoln	402.476.6644
Joe Voda's Drum City	Omaha	402.397.1060

NEVADA

Area Code 702

Bizarre Guitar	Reno	702.331.1001
Carpenters Music World	Reno	702.852.7618
Desert Music	Las Vegas	702.363.3333
Mahoney's Pro Music & Drum Las Vegas		702.382.9147
Modern Guitar	Reno	702.825.1982
Vesely Music	Las Vegas	702.382.8777

equip.
91
svcs.

R E T A I L

NEW HAMPSHIRE

Area Code 603

Blue Mountain Guitar	.W. Labanon	603.298.5829
Daddy's Junky Music	. . . . .Salem	603.893.6635
Daddy's Junky Music	.Portsmouth	603.436.1142
Daddy's Junky Music	. . .Nashua	603.888.1160
Daddy's Junky Music	.Manchester	603.669.9346
Downtown Dave's	. . . .Lebannon	603.448.4813
E.U. Wurlitzer Music	. . . .Nashua	603.888.8333
E.U. Wurlitzer Music	. . . . . .Salem	603.898.3287

NEW JERSEY

Area Code 609

Fiocchi's Drum Studio	. .Vineland	609.691.0213
Sam Ash Music	. . . . . .Cherry Hill	609.667.6696
The Music Place	. . . . .Berlin	609.768.2226

Area Code 908

Dave Phillips Music	. .Phillipsburg	908.454.3313
Delucia's Marching Emporium Little Silver	. . . .	908.219.0400
Monmouth Music	. . . . .Red Bank	908.747.8888
Pianos Plus	. . . . .Greenbrook	908.752.8282
Sam Ash Music	. . . . .Edison	908.572.5595
South Jersey Drum	. .Tom's River	908.286.9800

Area Code 973

Glenn Weber Drum	. . . .W. Orange	973.736.3113
O'DiBella Music	. . . . .Bergenfield	973.385.5800
Sam Ash Music	. . . . . . .Paramus	973.843.0119
Spinosa Music	. . . . .Belleville	973.751.5666

R E T A I L

NEW MEXICO

Area Code 505

All One Tribe Drums . . . . . . .Taos   800.444.Drum

Allegro Music . . . . .Santa Fe   505.471.9112

Hubbard's Music . . . .Las Cruces   505.526.8884

Luchetti Drum . . . . .Albuquerque   505.298.5519

Taos Drums
PO Box 1916 So. Santa Fe Rd., Taos NM 87571
P: 800.655.6786/ 505.758.6786 **F:** 505.758.9844
Hrs: M-Sat: 9-6, Sun: 11-6
Venues served: Taos, Sante Fe, Albuquerque
vicinity. **Svcs:** Ship anywhere, UPS.
Brand lines: Taos Native Amer. style drumsets &
drums. Also djembes, ashikos & ashebes.

Woody Hand Perc. . . . . .Taos   505.758.9825

NEW YORK

Area Code 212

Drummers World . . . . .NYC   212.840.3057

Manny's . . . . .NYC   212.819.0576

Modern Drum Shop . . . . . . .NYC   212.575.8893

Sam Ash Music . . . . .NYC   212.398.6044

Area Code 315

A&A Drum Ctr. . . . . .Utica   315.724.5080

Big Apple . . . . . . .New Hartford   315.732.4162

Drum Studio . . . . .Syracuse   315.463.8965

Rhythms . . . . .Fayetteville   315.637.2202

Area Code 516

Long Island Drum Ctr. . .Plainview   516.694.5432

Long Island Drum Ctr. . .Medford   516.758.6868

Long Island Drum Ctr. . .Commack   516.499.0455

Sam Ash . . . . .Huntington Stn   516.421.9333

Sam Ash . . . . .Carle Place   516.333.8700

R E T A I L

NEW YORK cont'd

Area Code 518

Daddy's Junky Music . . . .Albany   518.452.9431

Drome Sound . . . . .Schenectady   518.370.3701

Only Guitar Shop . . . .Clifton Park   518.371.1232

Area Code 607

Bearfoot Perc. . . . . . .Prattsburgh   607.522.4550

Toko Imports
215 N. Cayuga St. Ithaca, NY 14850
P: 800.560.3786 **P/F:** 607.277.3780
Web: http://www.gateways.com/ithaca/toko/
Hrs: M-Th: 11 - 5:30, F: 11 - 6, Sat: 10:30 - 5
Other hrs by appt only. **Venues served:** Grass Roots
Festival(July), Trumansburg, N.Y. same day svc. avail.
Svcs: catalogs, mail order, UPS. **Brand lines:** LP,
Remo, Earth Rhythm, Final Chants, many others.

Area Code 716

Afena Akoma . . . . .Brockport   800.98.Afena

Buffalo Drum Outlet . . . . . .Buffalo   716.897.0950

Costello's Music . . . . . . .Fredonia   716.672.5176

Daddy's Junky Music . . . .Buffalo   716.835.0516

Area Code 718

Musician's General Store
Brooklyn 718.596.4962

Percussion Paradise
Staten Island 718.667.3777

Royal Music World . . . . .Flushing   718.358.8848

Sam Ash . . . . .Forest Hills   718.793.7983

Sam Ash . . . . .Brooklyn   718.951.3888

School for Musical Performance
910 Kings Highway Brooklyn, NY 11223
P: 718.339.4989 **F:** 718.339.4989
Svcs: mail order, UPS. **Brand lines:** We buy,
sell, trade new & used drums, mallet instruments,
perc. instruments, accessories, hardware, cymbals & cases. Consignment instruments wel-
come. **See Coupon Section for $avings**.

R E T A I L

NEW YORK cont'd

Area Code 914

Long Island Drum Ctr.	Nyack	914.358.5303
Sam Ash Music	White Plains	914.949.8448

NORTH CAROLINA

Area Code 704

Drums & Co.	Charlotte	704.566.6045
Music & Arts Ctr.	Charlotte	704.341.0000
Music Mart	Concord	704.782.6013
Musician's Workshop	Asheville	704.252.1249
Reliable Music	Charlotte	704.375.8662

Area Code 864

Parker Music	Greenville	864.292.2920

Area Code 910

McFadyn Music	Jacksonville	910.353.1451
Music Barn	Greensboro	910.272.2118
Talking Drum	Greensboro	910.273.7470

Area Code 919

2112 Perc.	Raleigh	919.833.0046
C B Ellis Music	Burlington	919.228.1709
Carver Music	Washington	919.975.1030
Music Connection	Raleigh	800.334.6770
Music Loft	Carboro	919.968.4411
Music Loft	Durham	919.286.9539
Music Loft	Raleigh	919.872.0331

R E T A I L

NORTH DAKOTA

Area Code 701

Eckroth Music . . . . .Bismarck   701.223.6707

Ficek Music Mart . . . . .Dickinson   701.225.8906

OHIO

Area Code 216

Daybreak Band Instr.& Rpr
Cortland 216.637.6014

Educators Music . . . . .Lakewood   216.226.6166

Falls Music Ctr. . .Cuyahoga Falls   216.928.2157

Gattuso's Music Ctr. . . . . .Canton   216.456.2806

Guitar Ctr. . . . . .N. Olmstead   216.777.7900

Lentine Music . . . .Richmond Hts.   216.791.2700

Lentine Music . . . . . . .Cleveland   216.741.1400

Area Code 330

Lentine Music . . . . .Akron   330.434.3138

The Drum Shop . . . . . . .Struthers   330.755.9463

Area Code 419

Full Score Music . . . . .Toledo   419.473.0555

LG Sound & Drums . . . . . .Toledo   419.472.5323

Peeler Music & Sound . . . .Toledo   419.385.0009

Tri-State Music . . . . .Bryan   419.636.6996

Area Code 513

Dayton Band Instrument . .Dayton   513.275.7771

Drumshine Shop . . . . .Cincinnati   513.821.8866

Shaw's Music Ctr. . . . .Centerville   513.436.5800

R E T A I L

Area Code 614

Columbus Pro Perc.	Columbus	614.885.7372
Denver Greenlee Band Instr. Circleville		614.474.4571
Percussion Concepts	Mt. Vernon	614.392.1888
Williams Perc.	Columbus	614.272.1303

Area Code 937

Ace Music Super Store	Dayton	937.253.4318
Hauer Music	Dayton	937.222.2815

OREGON

Area Code 503

African Rhythm Traders	Portland	503.288.6950
Apple Music	Portland	503.226.0036
Cedar Mountain Drums	Portland	503.235.6345
Horsehoe Music	Portland	503.245.8442
Larry's Music	Grants Pass	503.476.4525
Musicians Friend	Medford	503.772.8366
Musicians Outlet	Medford	503.317.5707
The Drum Shop	Portland	503.771.7789
The Flam Trap	Salem	503.364.6702
Wally's Music Shop	Oregon City	503.656.5323
Whethers Music	Salem	503.362.8708

Area Code 541

Albany Music & Sound	Albany	541.967.8293

R E T A I L

PENNSYLVANIA

Area Code 215

George's Music . . . . . Feasterville   215.357.6610

George's Music . . . . . . Nth Wales   215.699.4040

Philadelphia Music . . . . Bensalem   215.639.9952

Pro Drum & Percussion
363 North Easton Rd. Glenside, PA 19038
P: 215.887.1462 **F:** 215.887.3793
Venues served: Keswick Theater
Svcs: Same day delivery Avail.
Brand lines: Largest selection of exotic & traditional percussion instruments on the planet.

Steve Weiss Music . . Philadelphia   215.329.1639

Zapf's Music . . . . Philadelphia   215.924.8736

Area Code 412

Brighton Music Ctr. . . . Pittsburgh   412.821.5908

Drum World . . . . Pittsburgh   412.343.2600

Pianos-N-Stuff . . . . . . Pittsburgh   412.828.1003

Swissvale Music . . . . Pittsburgh   412.351.5882

Wadells Drum Ctr . . . . Leechburg   412.845.3786

Area Code 610

California Drum Shop . . Bethlehem   610.866.5418

Earth Rhythms . . . . . . W. Reading   610.374.3730

George's Music . . . . Berwyn   610.640.0777

George's Music . . . . . Springfield   610.543.2553

George's Music . . . . . Spring City   610.948.0780

Medley Music . . . . . . Bryn Mawr   610.527.3090

Percussion Educational Services
404 W. State Street Media, PA 19063
P/F: 610.892.4742
Eml: duoselah@mindspring.com
Hrs: M-F: 2 - 8 Sat: 10 - 2
Special svcs: Ship anywhere via UPS.
Brand lines: All major brands.

R E T A I L

Area Code 610 cont'd

Rosewood Music . . . . . .Emmaus   610.965.9211

Sam Ash . . . . . . .King of Prussia   610.265.6444

Area Code 717

Dale's Drum Shop
4440 Fritchey St. Harrisburg, PA 17109
P: 717.652.2466 **F:** 717.652.3694
Hrs: M-F: 11 - 8, Sat: 11 - 5 Sun.- Closed
Venues served: Hershey Park Arena, Harrisburg Forum, HBG City Island w/ same day delivery avail.
Svcs: catalog, mail order, UPS.
Brand lines: DW, Tama, Pearl, Yamaha, Ludwig, Fibes, Sonor, Mapex, Zildjian, Sabian, Paiste.

Drums Etc.
253 North Queen Street Lancaster, PA 17603
P: 800.922.3786/ 717.394.3786 **F:** 717.394.5226
Hrs: M-F: 12 - 8:30, Sat: 12 - 6 Sun.- Closed
Svcs: catalogs, mail order, UPS.
Brand lines: Tama, Pearl, Ludwig, LP, Zildjian, Sabian, Gibralter, Roland, Paiste.

Jim's Drum Shop . . . . .Highspire   717.939.1048

Terrace Music Ctr. . . . . .Pottsville   717.544.6300

Wray Music House . . . .Lemoyne   717.761.8222

Area Code 814

Let There Be Drums . . . . .Erie   814.453.5933

RHODE ISLAND

Area Code 401

Al Drew Drum Shop . .Woonsocket   401.769.3552

Axelrod Music . . . . .Warwick   401.421.4833

Daddy's Junkie Music . .Warwick   401.823.3239

Ross Music . . . .North Providence   401.726.8060

Ross Music . . . . .Warwick   401.738.7677

Twin City Music . . . . .Providence   401.943.2622

R E T A I L

SOUTH CAROLINA

Area Code 803

Draisen-Edwards	Anderson	803.225.4666
Eastside Guitar & More Greenville		803.458.8220
Fox Music	Charleston	803.571.7744
Hames Music	Gaffney	803.489.1166
Pecknel Music	Greenville	800.868.2275
Sim's Music	Columbia	803.772.3966
TNT Music Inc.	Clemson	803.654.3697

Area Code 864

Newell's Music	Greenwood	864.223.5757
Palmetto Music	Greenville	864.232.1726

Area Code 605

Haggerty's Musicworks Rapid City		605.348.6737
Mollet Music	Yankton	605.665.7676
Sioux Falls Music	Sioux Falls	605.334.5361
Taylor Music	Aberdeen	605.225.1335

Check out the inside back cover to order a T-Shirt

RETAIL

TENNESSEE

Area Code 423

Bandland Horns & Perc. .Knoxville   423.675.6588

Payne's Music Ctr. . . . . .Knoxville   423.531.1988

Area Code 615

Fork's Drum Closet . . . .Nashville   615.383.8343

Guitar Heaven . . . . .Nashville   615.833.8483

Klassy Keys Music Studio
Clarksville 615.647.0166

Musicians Wholesale Club
Nashville 615.832.7450

Pro Percussion . . . . . . .Nashville   615.244.3786

Area Code 901

Chandler Music . . . . . .McKenzie   901.352.2215

Drum Supply House . . . .Jackson   901.423.3786

Memphis Drum Shop . .Memphis   901.276.2328

Strings and Things . . . .Memphis   901.278.0500

TEXAS

Area Code 210

Hermes Music . . . . .Pharr   210.781.8472

Hermes Music . . . . .San Antonio   210.734.5898

Kirk Scott Drum City . .San Antonio   210.656.4785

Area Code 214

Brook Mays . . . . .Dallas   214.631.0921

Area Code 281

Guitar Ctr. . . . . .N. Houston   281.537.9100

R E T A I L

TEXAS cont'd

Area Code 512

Drum Connection	Austin	512.832.5361
So. Texas Music Mart Corpus Christi		512.993.7866
Strait Music	Austin	512.476.6927
Tommy's Drum Shop	Austin	512.444.3786

Area Code 713

Drum, Keys & Guitar Ctr	Houston	713.781.3786
Guitar Ctr.	Houston	713.952.9070
Houston Perc. Ctr.	Houston	713.864.5050

Area Code 806

Jent's House of Music	Lubbock	806.795.5579

Area Code 817

C&S Music	Fort Worth	817.292.7614
Guitar Ctr.	Arlington	817.277.3510
Pepper of Dallas	Ft. Worth	800.345.6296

Area Code 903

Action Sound	Kilgore	903.884.4262

Area Code 915

Caldwell Music	Midland	915.697.0852
Caldwell Music	Abilene	915.677.2471
Caldwell Music	San Angelo	915.655.7381
Danny's Music Box	El Paso	915.593.1035
Kurland Salzman Music	El Paso	915.751.1219
Kurland-Salzman Music	El Paso	915.592.8207
Richie's Drum Exchange	El Paso	915.778.8818

Area Code 972

Guitar Center	Dallas	972.960.0011

equip.
103
svcs.

R E T A I L

UTAH

Area Code 801

Discount Music Ctr	Bountiful	801.292.8427
Entry Music Ctr.	St. George	801.673.0373
Music Village	Ogden	801.399.1418
Summerhays	Salt Lake City	800.345.6296
Wagstaff Music	Salt Lake City	801.261.4555

VERMONT

Area Code 802

Advance Music	Burlington	802.863.8652
Fallers Music	Bennington	802.442.4977
Michael's Music	Rutland	802.773.0105
Play It Again Sam	Montpelier	802.229.0295

VIRGINIA

Area Code 703
Capone Music	Annandale	703.256.5200

Area Code 757
Alpha Music	Virginia Beach	757.486.2001
Audio Light & Musical	Norfolk	757.853.2424

Area Code 804
Boykins Music	Williamsburg	804.229.1916
Calamas Musical	Norfolk	804.622.2148
Southern Music	Richmond	804.270.9565

RETAIL

WASHINGTON

Area Code 206

American Music	Seattle	206.633.1774
Band Aid Music	Bellview	206.462.0288
Drum Exchange	Seattle	206.545.3564
Drum Garage	Seattle	206.363.4494
Drums Northwest	Kent	206.946.0338
Green River Music	Auburn	206.833.2240
Hugo Helmer Music	Mt. Vernon	206.336.6109
John's Music	Seattle	206.548.0916
Music 6000	Olympia	206.786.6000
Purvis Drum Shop	Seattle	206.244.0550
Seattle Drum Shop	Seattle	206.363.1853
Tacoma Drum Shop	Tacoma	206.584.8130
Ted Brown Music	Tacoma	800.345.6296

Area Code 360

Beacock's Music	Vancouver	360.694.7134
Cascade Music	Marysville	360.659.8555
Ted Brown Music	Silverdale	360.692.4030

Area Code 509

Hoffman Music	Spokane	509.328.3888
Spokane Drum Ctr.	Spokane	509.482.1989
The Drum Guy	Spokane	509.838.1646

WEST VIRGINIA

Area Code 304

De Vincent's Music	Morgantown	304.292.3356
Don Elkins Music	Logan	800.752.4573
Gorby's Music	South Charleston	304.744.9452
Pied Piper	Huntington	800.995.6874

R E T A I L

WISCONSIN

Area Code 414

Cascio Music Co.
13819 W. National Ave, New Berlin WI 53151
P: 414.789.7600 **F:** 414.786.6840
Hrs: M-F: 10-8PM Sat: 10-4PM
Venues served: Marcus Amph., Bradley Ctr.,
Marcus Ctr. for Perf Arts, Alpine Valley Music
Theater. w/ same day delivery avail.
Svcs: Ship anywhere UPS, RPS, DHL
Brand lines: All major brands of drum & perc
eqp. Call for catalog

GW Music . . . . .West Bend   414.334.4426

Heid Music . . . . .Appleton   414.734.1969

Henri's Music . . . . . . .Green Bay   414.496.3710

Interstate Musician
PO Box 510865, New Berlin WI 53151
P: 800.In-A-Band **F:** 414.786.6840
Eml: musician@execpc.com
Web: www.http://execpc.com/~musician
Venues served: Marcus Amph., Bradley Ctr.,
Marcus Ctr. for Perf Arts, Alpine Valley Music
Theater. w/ same day delivery avail.
Svcs: Mail order. Ship anywhere UPS, RPS, DHL.
Brand lines: All major brands of drum & perc eqp.
Call for catalog

Tony's Drum Shop . . . . .Appleton   414.731.3309

Uncle Bob's Music . . .Milwaukee   414.453.2700

White House of Music . .Waukesha   414.798.9700

Area Code 608

Drums n' Moore . . . . . . .Monona   608.222.Drum

Great Northern Music . . .Madison   608.231.5992

Ward-Brodt . . . . .Madison   800.369.6255

Area Code 715

Jim Laabs Music . . .Stevens Point   715.341.1666

R E T A I L

USED/VINTAGE

A Drummer's Tradition
San Rafael . . . . .CA   415.458.1688

Al Drew's Drum Shop
Woonsocket . . . . .RI   401.769.3552

Amanda's Texas Underground
Annapolis . . . . .MD   301.261.2888

American Vintage Drums
Grant Pass . . . . .OR   541.474.2667

Blair-N-Drums
Grand Rapids . . . . .MI   800.733.8164

C & C Drum Shop
Kansas City . . . . .MO   816.468.1919

Colorado Drum & Perc.
Ft. Collins . . . . .CO   970.229.9473

Columbus Percussion
Columbus . . . . .OH   800.775.7372

Dr. Sound USA
NYC . . . . .NY   212.334.5478

Drum Ctr. of Indianapolis
Indianapolis . . . . .IN   317.594.8989

Explorer's Percussion
Kansas City . . . . .MO   816.KC.Drums

Fitzco-Products Ltd.
Schenectady . . . . .NY   518.374.0251

Guitars Unlimited Music Ctr.
Bridgeport . . . . .CT   203.331.0040

John Gill's Vintage Drums
Seaford . . . . .NY   516.783.9196

Jollity Drum Farm
Coach Road Box 2324, Argyle NY 12809
P: 518.638.8559
Specialty: Bobby Chiasson offers a vintage mail
order list with a focus on the 1960's. Rogers our
specialty. **Svcs:** Buy, Sell, & Trade. Ship USPS,
UPS, Emory Worldwide. Visa, & Mastercard accept-
ed. **See coupon section for $avings**

King Louie Music
Carlisle . . . . .PA   717.258.1177

King's Corner
Annapolis . . . . .MD   410.280.2952

Lou Rose Music
Edison . . . . .NJ   908.985.3333

USED/VINTAGE

Memphis Drum Shop
Memphis . . . . .TN   901.276.Beat

Music Manor
Lansing . . . . .MI   517.393.5995

Old Timers
Cincinnati . . . . .OH   513.791.1993

Orange County Drum & Perc.
R.S.M. . . . . .CA   714.589.7308

Palmetto Music
Greenville . . . . .SC   864.232.1726

Percussion Instrument Exchange
22 Jemison RD., Rochester NY 14623 - 2014
P: 716.436.7630 **F:** 716.436.7640
Eml: brianrep@frontiernet.net
Specialty: Specializing in buying & selling Mallet
instruments & Timpani.

Pro Percussion
Nashville . . . . .TN   800.241.Drum

Rebeats Vintage Drums
Alma . . . . .MI   517.463.4757

Rockin' Ritas Recycled Drums & Perc.
9640 Mission Gorge Rd. # B285 Santee CA 92071
P/F: 619.596.4627
Speciatly: Used drums, cymbals, stands etc.
Svcs: Mail order catalog. Fedex & UPS svc. avail.
Call for latest list.

Rockin' Robin: Drum Zone
Houston . . . . .TX   713.529.5442

Romper's Relics
Milton . . . . .Ontario   905.876.2338

Sandusky Music
Sandusky . . . . .OH   419.626.6060

Skins and Tins
Champaign . . . . .IL 217.352.Drum

Song Bird Music
Ottawa . . . . .Ontario   613.594.5323

Tex's Phoenix Underground
. . . . .TX   210.342.8309

The Starving Musician
Santa Clara . . . . .CA   408.554.9041

Top Cat Percussion
Kansas City . . . . .MO   913.782.2174

Vintage Drum Ctr.
Libertyville . . . . .IA   800.729.3111

equip.
109
svcs.

INT'L RETAIL

AUSTRALIA

Drum Centre Warehouse
Petersham 02.9564.2566

Drum City . . . . Sydney 02.9281.0255

Drum Worx . . . . . . Fortitude Valley 07.3252.4629

Drummers Warehouse
Bowen Hills 07.3252.1232

Gold Coast Music . . . . . Southport 07.5532.7100

Main Street Music
Greensborough Vic 03.9434.7041

CANADA

Anderson Music
Medicine Hat, Alberta 403.526.5306

Italmélodie . . . . .Montreal   514.273.3224

Italmélodie . . . . .Chomedey-Laval   514.681.4131

Musique Daniel Coté
Trois Riviéres 819. 691.0071

Musique Richard Gendreau
Quebec 418. 522.3877

Steve's Music Store . . . . . .Montreal   514. 395.8931

CARIBBEAN

Angitua

Hallpikes Store . . . . . .St. Johns   809.461.0534

The Map Store . . . . . . .St. Johns   809.462.5384

Bahamas

Edem Music Centre . . .Bahamas   809.325.5414

Grand Bahama Music & Rpr
Bahamas 809.352.9262

Maranatha Music Ctr . . . . .Nassau   809.325.4969

Ricardo Major Music Ctr. .Freeport   809.352.3444

Drum Tech . . . . .Hamilton   809.295.1759

Pianos Plus . . . . .Hamilton   809.295.8026

CARIBBEAN cont'd

Barbados
A&B Music Supply 809.427.5384

Dominican Republic
Musical Padilla
Rep.Dominicana 809.688.3066
Pro Musica S.A.
Gazcue Santo Domingo 809.476.7075

Grand Caymen Islands
C. Barnett Music
British West Indies 809.949.0303

Jamaica
Music Mart
Kingston 10W 809.926.4687
Sam Wisdon Music . . .Kingston 809.929.9188

Martinique
Live Music Enterprise
Ft de France 011.596.797.796
Symphony Antilles 011.596.606.454

Netherland Antilles
Rodrigues Music Ctr. . . . Antilles 011.599.961.4139
Zeelandia Music . . . . . .Curacao 011.599.961.4219

Puerto Rico
Bigio Casa de Musica .Caguas   809.743.2807
La Antorcha Music . . .Arecibo   809.878.6663
Margarida Music . . . . . .Rio Piedras 809.274.0440
Musikos . . . . .Humacao 809.850.5890
Polifonia . . . . .Hato Rey 809.758.4211
Pure Sound . . . . .Bayamon 809.798.3099
Taller de Musica . . . . .Yauco   809.856.8036
Taller Musical . . . . . . .Aguadilla 787.891.3102
Tropical Music . . . . . . .Santurce 809.726.5360
Villa Piano . . . . .Santurce 809.727.5050

Virgin Islands
Caribbean Music Supply
St. Croix 809.773.2222

EUROPE

Austria

Drumhouse . . . . .Altmunster 43.7612.882.8412
Key-Wi Music . . . . .Salzberg 43.662.82.2240
Musik Gattermann .Bad Hall 43.7258.4344

England

Andertons Music . . . .Surrey 44.014.833.8212
Birmingham Drum Centre . . 44.0121.778.3626
Carlsbro . . . . .Leicester 44.0116.262.4183
Carlsbro . . . . . .Nottingham 44.0115.958.1888
Carlsbro . . . . .Sheffield 44.0114.264.0000
Drum and Perc . . . .Dartford 44.0132.222.4449
Drum Bank Music .Bishopston 44.0117.975.5366
Drums Inc. . . . .Hornchurch 44.0170.847.8450
Electro Music . . . .Doncaster 44.0130.236.9999
Fret Music . . . . . . .Hampton 44.0170.377.4433
GIG Sounds . . . . . .London 44.0181.769.5681
Impact Percussion . .London 44.0171.403.5900
Johnny Roadhouse Music
Manchester 44.161.273.3069
Liverpool City Drum Ctr. 44.0151.236.4405
London Drum . . . . . .London 44.0181.690.1848
Mister Music . . . . .Glasgow 44.0141.429.6139
Modern Music . . . . . . .Truro 44.050.003.0405
Murray Seaton's Drum Ctr.
Edinburgh 44.0131.667.3844
Newcastle Drum Ctr Newcastle 44.0191.221.0301
Percy Prior's Music . . .Bucks 44.0149.444.3418
Pro Percussion . . . . .London 44.0171.485.4434
Rockbottom Drum Cavern
Surrey 44.0181.680.8134
Rosetti Limited . . . . . .Essex 44.0137.655.0033
Sound Attak . . . . .Essex 44.0120.679.1371
Soundhouse . . . .Gloucester 44.0145.241.7429
Soundhouse . . . . . .Hereford 44.014.241.7429
Stage One Drums . . . .Essex 44.0120.657.8975
Supreme Drums . . . .London 44.0181.520.3873
The Drum Shop .Gateshead 44.0191.495.0201
The Music Store . . . . .Surrey 44.0181.399.1166

EUROPE cont'd

The Northern Drum Centre Yorkshire	....	44.012.743.71271
The Rock Factory	. .W. Yorks	44.0197.751.3643
Underground Sounds	. .Kent	44.0189.253.3778
Wembley Drum Centre Middlesex	....	44.0181.795.4001

France

All Music	.........Le Havre	02.35.22.91.12
Andre Music	.........St. Lo	02.33.57.21.62
Annecy Musique	.....Annecy	04.50.51.03.50
Au Petite Noál	........Reims	03.26.47.36.25
Aux Guitares	.......Mulhouse	89.46.46.38
Batterie & Co.	.........Lille	03.20.12.00.70
Batterie Music	.......Nantes	02.40.71.75.73
Bemer Musique	........Metz	03.87.75.26.40
Bemer Musique	.....Thionville	82.59.29.20
Betbeder	...........Anglet	05.59.63.52.85
Boesche Musique	.....Colmar	89.41.24.59
Cagnes Music	.......Cagnes	04.92.02.73.94
Clinic Instrumental	.....Rouen	35.98.32.75
Compeigne Musque Compeigne	....	44.40.10.18
Custom Guitar	......St. Brieuc	02.96.61.75.75
Dreux Music	.........Dreux	37.42.18.14
Dussau	.............Pau	05.59.27.58.62
Floyd Music	.......Mauguio	04.67.20.00.85
Gebelin	..........Marseille	04.91.54.21.19
Gong Music	........Grenoble	04.76.87.48.16
Gur Music	..........Belfort	03.84.28.14.61
Hall de la Musique	.....Quimper	98.55.49.12
Hall Music	............Tours	02.47.20.32.60
Hamm	.............Paris	01.44.39.35.35
Hamm	.............Paris	01.43.25.91.84
Hamm	.............Cretieil	01.42.07.98.85
Hietz	................Lyon	04.78.37.46.23
Inforythmie	........Bordeaux	56.99.39.00
Jericho	...............Lille	20.15.92.78
Jim Music	..........Nantes	04.40.08.21.21

EUROPE cont'd

France cont'd

La Baguetterie	Toulouse	05.61.13.77.77
La Baguetterie	Rennes	02.99.30.10.20
La Baguetterie	Lyon	04.78.39.13.14
La Baguetterie	Paris	01.42.81.06.80
La Baguetterie	Frejus	04.94.44.23.58
La Baguetterie Strasbourg Neudorf		04.94.44.23.58
La Boite aux Rythmes	Paris	48.78.48.16
La Boite aux Rythmes	Paris	45.26.52.10
Le Musicien	Orleans	02.38.53.11.93
Maison Gatti	Nice	04.93.62.00.04
Martin jacques	Nevers	86.59.36.00
Mastrolilli	Douai	27.98.98.08
Melody Music	Caen	02.31.85.71.22
Michel Musique	Grenoble	76.46.58.82
Michenaud	Nantes	02.40.35.30.12
Moreau Music	Valenciennes	27.46.84.15
Music Box	Cannes	04.93.38.92.93
Music Center	Le Mans	43.75.55.26
Music Center	Albi	63.54.73.58
Music City	Aytre	05.46.45.22.22
Music Forum	St. Savine	03.25.79.80.99
Music France	Le Mans	02.43.77.10.29
Music Hall	Clermont Ferrand	73.30.94.19
Music Hemann	Caen	31.82.61.94
Music Leader	Annecy	04.50.52.74.28
Music Market	Cavaillon	04.90.71.71.20
Music Melody	Alencon	02.33.26.73.36
Music Melody	Rouen	02.35.15.48.12
Music Plus	Marseille	04.91.48.94.42
Music Plus	Lyon	04.72.73.06.67
Music Shop	Aurillac	04.71.48.48.68
Musical	Nice	04.93.82.22.50
Musicofolies	Cognac	05.45.82.88.26
Musicstock	Tours	02.47.49.29.49
Musique 74	Annecy	04.50.67.42.56
Musique Limoges	Limoges	55.33.53.17
Musique Orange	Orange	04.90.34.16.21

EUROPE cont'd

France cont'd

Musique Shop	Strasbourg	03.88.36.33.58
Nouteau	Angers	41.87.55.01
Occ' Land	Paris	48.74.31.92
Orphee Music	Valence	04.75.56.34.20
Pansiot	Dijon	80.67.11.95
Paolin	Bergerac	53.57.27.38
Percussion Plus	Lyon	04.72.10.01.06
Pianoceane	Le Havre	35.43.06.39
Royez Musik	Amiens	22.91.03.21
S.O.S. Musique	Carcassonne	68.25.26.65
Scotto Musique	Marseille	04.91.37.58.65
Sevenant	Gourin	97.23.41.26
Sud Musique	Perpignan	04.68.51.31.14
Thevenet Music	Poitiers	05.49.41.21.31
Thevenet Music	Angouleme	05.45.95.33.82

Germany

Amptown	Hamburg	040.646.0040
ASCELL Vertrieb GmbH	Dolzig	0342.058.4436
ASCELL Vertrieb GmbH	Gotha	036.212.9353
Audio Tours	Recklinghausen	023.616.0840
Bayreuth	Hamburg	040.391.151
Berimbao - Percussion, Drums & more Reiderich		071.233.6543
Bernd Dorfner	Augsburg	082.141.6798
Cherry Musik	Braunschweig	053.133.9117
City-Music	Hamm	023.811.5076
Clyde's Musikladen	Bayreuth	092.151.2443
Czubak & Partner GbR—K Drums Ennepetal		023.337.2724
Dr. Drum	Weisbaden	0611.950.5022
Drum Center	Koln	0121.258.1277
Drum Ctr. Bochum	Bochum	023.27.3938
Drum Studio Bonn	Bonn	022.847.4943
Drum Studio Tittmann	Hamburg	040.439.1500
Drumline	Elmshorn	041.211.738
Drummer's Drums	Gottingen	055.192.020
Drummer's Focus	Munchen	089.273.1091

EUROPE cont'd

Germany cont'd

Drums & Musik	Zellingen	093.645.361
Drums Only	Frankfurt	069.442.089
Drums Only	Koblenz	026.183.011
Drums Only	Schorndorf	071.812.2126
Drums Pur	Neunkirchen	027.3577.3377
Ffortissimo	Fulda	066.174.447
Franky's Music	Konigswinter	022.448.3068
Groove Drums	Emsburen	059.039.3980
Guitar Place	Aschaffenberg	060.212.8180
House of Drums	Weisbaden	061.130.0202
In Sound	Kiel	043.166.5554
Lange Musikhaus	Ravensburg	075.12.779
Link's Musical Instruments	Hanau	061.812.3067
Live Lights Music	Munchen	089.5459.5810
Lyra Musikhaus	Munster	025.141.7090
Modern Drum Studio	Langenfeld	021.738.0542
Mr. Music	Donauworth	090.66.171
Music Center	Magdeburg	03.915.7857
Music Faire	Augsburg	082.159.4454
Music Store	Kaiserslautern	063.165.660
Music Store Professional	Koln	0221.9257.9130
Musik Borse	Garching	089.320.4499
Musik Center Feldmann	Rhede	0287.270.9192
Musik Kroger	Trier	065.149.261
Musik Land - Drum World Rosenheim		080.311.4429
Musik- & Pianohaus	Wurzburg	093.150.735
Musik Productiv Ibbenburen		0545.190.9140
Musik Schonstedt	Celle	05.141.6676
Musik-Markt	Muchen	089.503.061
Musikbox	Neuss	0213.127.4266
Musikhalle	Nurnberg	091.143.9900
Musikhaus Heintz	Xanten	028.014.483
Musikhaus Landry	Saarbrucken	068.181.2581
Musikhaus Musicant	Frankenthal	062.332.1777
Musikhaus "Polyhymnia"	Halle(saale)	034.530.445

EUROPE cont'd

Germany cont'd

Musikhaus Schultz Hohenst. Ernsttal   037.234.3731

Musikhaus Steiner . .Bremerhaven   047.147.164

Musikladen Bode . . . . . . .Itzehoe 048.216.2869

Musikladen Weiss . . . .Krumbach 082.826.1777

Percussion Center - Thomas Spindler
Bamberg 09.515.8353

Piano-Frey Musikhaus . .Heidenhiem   073.212.0881

PPC MUSIC . . . . .Hannover 051.132.4232

Professional Equipment . . .Ratingen 021.028.1049

Profitronic . . . . .Kassel   05.611.6715

Pulse Percussion . . . . .Berlin 030.623.3794

Reinhard Huttinger's ROCKHOUSE
Ansbach 098.164.650

Rock Shop . . . . .Karlsruhe 072.197.8550

Rock-Shop . . . . .Bochum 023.453.4626

Sandner Music Warehouse
Limburg/Lahn 06.431.3098

Second Hand Music Shop
Leverkusen 021.714.6046

Seidel + Partner GmbH
Wuppertal 020.245.2907

Session Drums . . . . . . .Walldorf   062.276.030

Snare Drum Studio . . . . .Bottrop 020.416.7963

Sound Drumland . . . . .Berlin 030.884.3030

Sound Land . . . . .Waiblingen 071.515.3091

Soundhaus Lubeck . . . . .Lubeck   045.178.984

Thomann Musikhaus .Burgebrach 095.469.2230

Top Sound . . . . .Bremen 042.165.5409

Troyan Instruments . . . .Munchen   089.267.421

Uli's Musik - Rock & Roll Equip.
Leverkusen 0214.876.0644

Willy's Rhythm-Shop . .Weisbaden 061.137.7153

Holland

Dijkman Muziek . . . . .Amsterdam 020.626.19.28

Eindhoven Musical . . .Eindhoven 040.2113995

Fentex . . . . .Badhoevedorp 020.659.4442

Muller Muziek . . . . . .Amsterdam 020.624.8592

Mueziek Hakkert . . . . .Rotterdam 010.413.0860

Italy

Bandiera	Italy	06.481.8435
Be-Bop Strumenti Musicali	Italy	06.970.2418
Carota Bruna	Pescara	085.421.3360
Casa Del Pianoforte	Pavia	03.823.3256
Casa Musicale Scavino	Snc.Torino	011.669.8118
Centro Musicale	Parma	052.177.2403
Cherubini	Rome	06.43.6971
Dori Il Box	Italy	06.930.4486
Drum Center	Galatina	083.656.1692
Drum Store	San Paolo	088.239.3200
Giocondi Strumenti Musicali Ascoli Piceno		073.626.0969
S. Benedetto Del Tront		073.559.4557
Il Pianoforte Snc	Trani (BA)	08.834.1052
K.F. Strumenti Musicali	Milano	024.895.2882
Loveri Guiseppe	Napoli	08.145.0279
M. Parise Strumenti Musicali	Prato	057.458.0203
M.V. Di Rosa Sberno	Catania	09.543.8674
Music Shop	S.Guistina (BL)	043.794.0432
Musicali Rossoni & Figli Srl	Trieste	04.036.7511
Musicarte srl	Rome	06.324.1741
Piparo Sas	Messina	09.051.558
Plaschke Srl	Bolzano	047.197.7274
Pro Musica Srl	Alessandria	013.122.2076
RAF Srl	Busto Arsizio (VA)	033.162.3255
Scaramuzza Strumenti	Cremona	037.243.4878
Sonora Snc.	Latina	077.369.4222
Sperati & F.	Savona	019.824.849
Timba-scuola di batteria e perc.Rome		06.556.6099
Titan Music S.A.	Aquaviva	054.990.1011
Zin Guglielmo Snc	Padova	049.876.0591

Spain

Real Musical, S.A.	Madrid	N/A

Switzerland

Drums Only	Zurich	041.1242.3942
Drumschool + Perc Shop	Basel	0041.61.271.7487
Musik Hug AG	Zurich	0041.125.16850

LATIN AMERICA

Argentina
Distrib. Cadara . . Vincente Lopez 541.797.2157
Netto . . . . .Buenos Aires 541.381.0154
Ricordi Americana .Buenos Aires 541.476.3452

Bolivia
Audio Watts . . . . .La Paz 591.231.5590
Sirex Ltda. . . . . .La Paz 591.235.4314

Brazil
Casa Vitale . . . . .Sao Paolo 5511.604.2024
Fermata Do Brasil . . . .Sao Paolo 5511.229.3411
Musicas Oscar Arany Ltda. . .Rio 5521.220.7601
Tower Music . . . . .Sao Paulo 5511.292.8371

Chile
Casa de Musica . . . . . . .Santiago 562.235.8079
Flora Mac Donald e Hijos .Santiago 562.223.8401

Colombia
Casa Musical Humberto Conti .Bogota .571.342.9520
Ortiza Ltda. . . . . .Bogota 571.248.1452

Costa Rica
Juan Bansbach Instr. . . .San Jose 506.222.8686
Pro Musica S.A. . . . . . . .San Jose 506.224.8898

El Salvador
Electronica 2001 . . .San Salvador 503.222.8783
Omni Music . . . . . .San Salvador 503.274.1368

Mexico
Mundo de la Musica . .Cuyoacan 525.554.9653
Pianos y Organos . .Cuauhtemoc 525.546.0811
Repertorio Wagner . . .Col Centro 525.510.1465
Veerkamp. . . . . .Col Roma 525.207.4687

Panama
Compania Alfaro . . .Panama City 507.223.0292

Paraguay
Musicshop . . . . .Asuncion 5952.121.4073

Peru
Anders & Harth Inst. Musicales.Lima 511.241.6327
Intermusica . . . . .Lima 511.432.8960

Uraguay
Palacio de la Musica .Montevideo 5982.920.919
Todo Musica . . . . . .Montevideo 5982.422.333

Venezuela
Hemisfero Musical . . . . .Caracas 582.762.0393
Pina Musical C.A. . . . . . .Caracas 582.482.6343

R E N T A L

CALIFORNIA

Centerstaging . . . . .Burbank 818.559.4333

Classic Equip. Rentals
Sherman Oaks 213.467.3432

Dr. Faws Drum Works
San Francisco 415.258.0894

Drum Doctors . . . . . .N. Hollywood 818.506.8123

Drum Paradise . . . . .N. Hollywood 818.762.7878

Ontario Music . . . . .Ontario 909.983.3551

Paul Jamieson Studio Rentals
Studio City 818.762.5759

Pro Piano . . . . .L.A. 310.474.2216

Pro Piano . . . . .San Francisco 415.621.1210

Rock-It Cargo . . . . .San Francisco 415.875.6880

Studio Instrument Rentals (SIR)
San Francisco 415.863.8200

Vintage Studio Rentals
Van Nuys 818.994.4849

R E N T A L

CALIFORNIA cont'd

Studio Instrument Rentals (SIR)
6465 Sunset Blvd., Hollywood CA 90028
P: 213.957.5460 **F:** 213.957.5472
Hrs: 7 days a wk M-F 7am-Midnight Sat-Sun 9-5
Eml: staff@sirny.com **Web:** sirny.com
Venues Served: Univ. Amph,The Greek, Hollywood
Bowl, all local clubs, TV & Movie.
Special Svcs: Same day deliv avail. 7 days a wk.
Yamaha, Pearl, DW, Mapex, Fibes, GMS, Remo,
Prem., LP, Toca. Also vintage and exotic drums.

FLORIDA

Downtown Sound of Orlando 407.297.7445

IRC . . . . .Ft Lauderdale 954.583.1030

R E N T A L

GEORGIA

Atlanta Pro Percussion . . . .Atlanta   770.436.378

HAWAII

Rocket Shells . . . . .Paia 808.575.9351

ILLINOIS

Midwest Inst. Rentals . . . .Chicago 312.227.3737

NEW JERSEY

SST . . . . .Weehawken 201.864.5666

NEW MEXICO

Taos Drums
PO Box 1916 So. Santa Fe Rd., Taos NM 87571
P: 800.655.6786/ 505.758.6786 **F:** 505.758.9844
Venues Served: Santa Fe/ Albuquerque/ Taos
vicinity. Reasonable rental. **Spcl svcs:** Technical
support available. Taos Native Amer. style drumsets
& drums. Also djembes, ashikos & ashebes.

NEW YORK

Big Mike Productions . . . . . . .NYC 212.971.7505

Carroll Music Instrument Serv. .NYC 212.868.4120

Complete Music . . . . .NYC 212.971.3150

Pro Piano . . . . .NYC 212.206.8794

Repaircussion Rentals
22 Jemison RD., Rochester NY 14623 - 2014
P: 716.436.7630 **F:** 716.436.7640
Eml: brianrep@frontiernet.net
Svcs: Western New York's leading concert
percussion rental business specializing in mallet
instruments & Timpani.

equip.
122
svcs.

R E N T A L

Studio Instrument Rentals (SIR)
520 W. 25 St. NYC 10001
P: 212.627.4900 **F:** 212.627.7079
Hrs: Mon- Sun 7am-12am
Eml: staff@sirny.com **Web:** sirny.com
Venues Served: MSG, Radio City, Beacon Thtr,
Bottom Line, Avery Fisher, Carnegie Hall, Tramps,
SOB's, Supper Club, Roseland. **Special Svcs:**
Same day deliv avail. 7 days a wk. Ship anywhere
fedex, UPS, airfreight. Catalog avail.Yamaha, Pearl,
DW, GMS, Remo, Prem., Tama, Slinger., LP, TOCA.

Toko Imports . . . . .Ithaca 800.560.3786

Toy Specialists . . . . .NYC 212.333.2206

PENNSYLVANIA

8th Street Music . . . . .Philadelphia 215.923.5040

Percussion Educational Svcs
404 W. State St. Media PA 19063
P/F: 610.892.4742
Eml: duoselah@mindspring.com
Hrs: M-F 2-8 Sat: 10-2
Venues Served: All Philadelphia, Sth Jersey,
Nthrn Delaware
Brand Lines: Toca, Giannini Swiss Drums,
Mapex, Ross, CB.

TENNESSEE

Drum Paradise Nashville . . . .Franklin 615.248.Drum

Studio Instrument Rentals (SIR)
1101 Cherry Ave. Nashville TN 37203
P: 615.255.4500 **F:** 615.255.4511
Hrs: Sunday- Saturday 8am-12am
Venues served: Ryman Aud., Starwood Amp,
Opry Land, studios in Nashville area.
Special Svcs: Same day delivery available.
Rental and studio setups. Pearl, Yamaha & LP.

WASHINGTON

American Music Rentals . . .Seattle 206.547.9609

CARTAGE

CALIFORNIA

METS—Musical Equip. & Transport Svcs.
Van Nuys 818.780.7711

Rock-It Cargo . . . . . .Los Angeles 310.410.0935

Studio Instrument Rentals (SIR)
L.A. 213.848.3660

Studio Instrument Rentals (SIR)
San Francisco 415.863.8200

FLORIDA

Downtown Sound of Orlando
3761 Silver Star Rd. Orlando 32808
P: 407.297.7445 **F:** 407.297.0996
Hrs: M-F 11am- 6pm
Special Svcs: Same day svc to venues possible.
Overnight service via Fedex available.
See ad pg

IRC . . . . .Ft Lauderdale 954.583.1030

GEORGIA

Rock-It Cargo . . . . . .College Park 404.669.0727

ILLINOIS

Big City Travel . . . . .Chicago 312.282.4333

Rock-It Cargo . . .Elk Grove Village 708.640.7625

NEW JERSEY

SST . . . . .Weehawken 201.864.5666

CARTAGE

NEW YORK

Rock-It Cargo . . . . .Valley Stream 516.825.7356

Sound Storage Inc. . . . . .NYC 212.243.6118

Studio Instrument Rentals . . .NYC 212.627.4900

Toy Specialists . . . . .NYC 212.333.2206

TENNESSEE

Rock-It Cargo . . . . .Nashville 615.256.7831

Studio Instrument Rentals
Nashville 615.255.4500

TEXAS

Threshold Sound & Magic
Lewisville 214.315.1609

REPAIR SERVICES

CUSTOMIZING & REPAIR

Bailes African Drumworks
7816 Cryden Way, Forestville MD 20747
P: 301.736.4708/ 800.861.Drum **F:** 301.736.7721
Web: BAILESADW@AOL.COM
See ad on pg 87 for more info.

Babylons End Perc. . . . . .KY 606.689.5275

Bill's Drum Rpr & Shell Shop . . .AL 205.533.3786

Case Instrument Repair . . . . . .OR 503.581.4676

Custom Drum Svcs . . . . .IN 219.482.7818

Cymbal Salvage
1126 So. Austin Blvd. #1W, Oak Park ILL 60304
P/F: 708.358.1716
Web: www.cymbalsalvage.com
We eliminate cracks & do customized drilling &
rivets. For more info send SASE or check out our
website. **See Coupon Section for $avings!**

Daybreak Band Instr.& Rpr . . .OH 216.637.6014

DLP Music & Repair . . . . .MI 313.581.4340

Dr. Faws Drum Works . . . . . . .CA 415.258.0894

Drum Doctors . . . . .CA 818.506.8123

Hit Drum Customizing . . . . .IL 630.585.0069

J&J Drum Restoration . . . . . . .OH 513.451.1680

La Drummerie . . . . .Montreal 514.892.4183

Mark Bedrossian Inst Repair . . .RI 401.467.6016

Midwest Custom Drum Repair . .IL 815.643.2514

Percussion Craftsman . . . . . . .TN 645.885.2128

Repaircussions
22 Jemison RD., Rochester NY 14623 - 2014
P: 716.436.7630 **F:** 716.436.7640
Eml: brianrep@frontiernet.net
Since 1979. Every conceivable percussion
instrument service except bar tuning. Thousands of
satisfied customers in every US State & Canadian
province & 57 countries worldwide.

Sputnick Drums . . . . .CA 415.334.4574

Taos Drums . . . . .NM 800.655.6786

RESTORATION SUPPLIES

Bill's Drum Rpr & Shell Shop . . .AL 205.533.3786
Drum Supply House . . . . .AL 901.423.3786
Midwest Custom Drum Repair . .IL 815.643.2514
Super Gloss Drum Material . . . .AZ 602.279.4041

Education

UNIVERSITIES/
SCHOOLS/
PRIVATE
INSTRUCTION

MIXED MEDIA

PROGRAMS

DRUM CIRCLES

ORGANIZATIONS

EDUCATION

ALABAMA

Colleges & Universities
Alabama State University 334.229.4341
Auburn University-Auburn 334.844.4165
Jacksonville State University 205.782.5559
N.E. ALA State Jr. College 205.228.6001
Samford University 205.870.2851
Snead State Jr. College 205.593.5120
Talladega College 205.362.0206
Troy State University 334.670.3281
Tuskegee University 205.727.8398
Univ. of Alabama- Brimingham 205.934.7375
Univ. of Alabama- Huntsville 205.895.6436
Univ. of Alabama- Tuscaloosa 205.348.7110
University of Montevallo 205.665.6670
University of North Alabama 205.760.4361
University of South Alabama 334.460.6136

ALASKA

Colleges & Universities
Univ. of Alaska- Anchorage 907.786.1595
Univ. of Alaska- Fairbanks 907.474.7555

ARIZONA

Colleges & Universities
Arizona State University 602.965.3371
Northern Arizona Univ. 520.523.3731
Phoenix College 602.285.7272
University of Arizona 520.621.1655

EDUCATION

ARKANSAS

Colleges & Universities

Arkansas State University	.501.972.2094
Arkansas Tech University	.501.968.0368
Henderson State University	.501.230.5036
Hendrix College	.501.329.6811
University of Arkansas	.501.575.4701
University of Arkansas	.501.569.3294
University of Arkansas	.501.460.1060
University of Central Arkansas	.501.450.3163
Williams Baptist College	.501.886.6741 x150

CALIFORNIA

Colleges & Universities

Ali Akbar College of Music	.415.454.6264
Calif. Institute of the Arts	.805.253.7817
Calif. State Univ.-Bakersfield	.805.664.3093
Calif. State Univ.-Fresno	.209.278.2654
Calif. State Univ.-Fullerton	.714.773.3511
Calif. State Univ.-Hayward	.510.881.3135
Calif. State Univ.-Long Bch	.310.985.4781
Calif. State Univ.-Los Angeles	.213.343.4060
Calif. State Univ.-Northridge	.818.885.3181
Calif. State Univ.-Sacramento	.916.278.6514
Calif. State Univ.-San Bernadino	.909.880.5859
Calif. State Univ.-Stanislaus	.209.667.3421
Cerritos College	.310.860.2451
Chabot College	.510.786.6829
Chaffey College	.909.941.2716
Chapman University	.714.997.6871
City College of San Francisco	.415.239.3641
Colege of Alameda	.415.522.7221
College of Notre Dame	.415.508.3597
Fresno City College	.209.442.4600
Fullerton College	.714.992.7000
Humboldt State University	.707.826.3531

CALIFORNIA cont'd

La Sierra University 909.785.2036
Long Beach City College 213.420.4309
Loyola Marymount Univ. 310.338.5154
Mills College 510.430.2171
Moorpark College 805.378.1443
Palomar College 619.744.1150 x2316
Pasadena City College 818.585.7208
Riverside Comm. College 909.222.8000
San Diego State University 619.594.6031
San Francisco Conservatory 415.564.8086
San Jose State University 408.924.4673
Santa Clara University 408.554.4428
Santa Monica College 310.452.9323
Sonoma State University 707.664.2324
Southwestern College 619.421.6700
Stanford University 415.723.3811
Univ. of Calif.-Irvine 714.856.6615
Univ.of Calif.-Los Angeles 310.825.4761
Univ. of Calif.-San Diego 619.534.3230
Univ. of La Verne 714.593.3511
Univ. of Southern Calif. 213.740.6935
Univ. of the Pacific 209.946.2415
Ventura College 805.654.6400
Whittier College 310.907.4237

Schools

Escola Nova de Samba 213.342.9336
LAMA 800.960.4175
PIT/ Musicians Institute 213.462.1384

Private Instruction

Rich Fongheiser
990-A Moraga Rd. Studio 6 Lafayette, CA 94549
P: 510.299.0709
Playing: 36 yrs **Teaching:** 26+ yrs drumset,
hand perc, concert perc. / classical, jazz, rock,
latin. **Level:** All.

EDUCATION

Private Instruction

Steve Houghton
1341 Cleveland Rd. Glendale CA 91202
P: 818.244.7970 **F:** 818.244.5820
Eml: SHPERC.
Teaching: drums & concert perc. / classical, jazz, rock, latin **Levels:** intermediate & advanced.

Rick Latham
PO Box 67306 Los Angeles, CA 90067
P: 310.281.9549 **F:** 818.989.0502
Eml: funkyrick@earthlink.net
Playing: 26 yrs all styles **Teaching:** 21 yrs drumset / jazz, rock, latin, linear concepts.
Levels: intermediate & advanced. Author of "Advanced Funk Studies" & "Contemporary Drumset Techniques".

Neil Sebba
8051 Willow Glen Rd Los Angeles, CA 90046
P: 213.654.8226 **Eml:** Nseb@aol.com
Playing: 19 yrs all styles. **Teaching:** 13 yrs drumset, concert perc., drum machine prog / classical, jazz, rock, latin, reggae. **Level:** all Professional, dedicated, patient. have own studio - W. LA & Bev. Hills loc. or make house calls. (See Coupon Section $avings).

Chuck Silverman
PO Box 572962 Tarzana CA 91357-2962
P: 818.609.1629 **F:** 818.609.9694
Eml: drumnart@sprynet.com
Web: http://www.chopshop.com/silverman/
Playing: 26 yrs all styles. **Teaching:** 17 yrs drumset, hand perc., timbales / jazz, rock, latin.
Level: intermediate & advanced.
World-renowned musician/ author/ educator.
A top authority on Afro-Caribbean drumming.

Paolo Mattioli - World Percussion Arts
115 S. Topanga Cyn. Blvd #169, Topanga CA 90290
P: 818.591.3111 **F:** 818.591.6756
Eml: drum1@pacificnet.net
Playing: 35 yrs all styles Teaching: 20 yrs Hand percussion -incl. djembe, & doundouns/ African & world beat. **Level:** All
Performed w/ Sting, Kenny Loggins, & Baba Olatunje.

EDUCATION

COLORADO

Colleges & Universities

Colorado Christian Univ. 303.202.0100

Colorado College 719.389.6545

Colorado State University 970.491.5529

Fort Lewis College 970.247.7447

Mesa State College 303.248.1427

Metropolitan State College 303.556.3180

Northeastern Jr. College 303.522.6600

Univ. of Colorado-Denver 303.556.2727

University of Denver 303.871.6400

Univ. of Northern Colorado 970.351.2678

CONNECTICUT

Colleges & Universities

Ctrl Connecticut State Univ. 860.832.2900

Connecticut College 203.439.2720

University of Bridgeport 203.576.4404

University of Connecticut 203.486.3728

University of Hartford 860.768.4454

Wstrn Connecticut State Univ. 203.837.8350

Yale University 203.432.1960

Private Instruction

Rob the Drummer
115 Montclair Drive W. Hartford, CT 06107-1266
P: 860.232.4044 **F:** 860.231.7470
Eml: Robtd@comix.com
Playing: 41 yrs jazz, rock. **Teaching:** 21 yrs
drumset. djembe, ashiko, congas, concert &
marching / classical, jazz, rock, latin, funk.
Level: all. Robert L. Gottfried, performing rock/
jazz drummer & recording artist. founder of "Rob
the Drummer" pro arts, pro sports, anti-sub-
stance abuse program. Has perf. at the White
House, Israel, Chernobyl, & Belgium

EDUCATION

DELAWARE

Colleges & Universities

University of Delaware 302.831.2577

DISTRICT OF COLUMBIA

Colleges & Universities

American University 202.885.3420
Catholic Univ. of America 202.319.5414
George Washington Univ. 202.994.6245
Levine School of Music 202.337.2227
Univ. of District of Columbia 202.274.5803

FLORIDA

Colleges & Universities

Bethune-Cookman College 904.255.1401
Broward Comm. College 954.475.6840
Broward Comm. College 305.973.2321
Eckerd College 813.867.1166x471
Florida A&M University 904.599.3334
Florida Atlantic University 407.367.3820
Florida Int'l University 305.348.2896
Florida Southern College 813.680.4217
Florida State University 904.644.3424
Harid Conservatory 407.997.2677
Hillsborough Comm. College 813.253.7684
Indian River Comm.College 407.468.4700
Miami-Dade Comm. Coll. Kendall . .305.237.2282
Miami-Dade Comm. Coll. N. 305.323.1450
Palm Beach Atlantic College 561.803.2000
Palm Beach Comm.College 407.439.8144
Rollins College 407.646.2233
Seminole Comm. College 407.328.2039
St. Petersburgh Jr. College 813.341.4360
Stetson University 904.822.8950

EDUCATION

Univ. of Central Florida 407.823.2869
Univ. of Miami 305.284.2241
Univ. of North Florida 904.646.2960
Univ. of South Florida 813.974.2311

Schools
The Players School of Music 800.724.4242

Private Instruction

Richard J. Bonenfant
3527 Eve court Orlando, FL 32810
P: 407.293.0111 **Pgr:** 407.372.6714 **F:** 407.297.7024
Playing: 41 yrs all styles
Teaching: 39 yrs drumset, concert & marching
perc. / classical, jazz, rock, latin. **Level:** all
3 yrs w/Naval Academy Band. 40 yrs exp w/comm.
rock, jazz, country groups, big bands, Las Vegas
prod shows, star shows & B'way shows.

GEORGIA

Colleges & Universities
Agnes Scott College 404.638.6259
Albany State College 912.430.4849
Armstrong State College 912.927.5325
Augusta College 706.737.1453
Berry College 706.232.5374
Brewton-Parker College 912.583.2241
Clark Atlanta University 404.880.8211
Clayton State College 404.961.3609
Columbus State College 706.568.2049
Darton College 912.430.6740
Dekalb College 404.299.4136
Emory University 404.727.6445
Georgia College 912.453.4226
Georgia Institute of Technology . . .404.894.3193
Georgia Southern University 912.681.5396
Georgia Southwestern College 912.931.2204

EDUCATION

Georgia State University 404.651.3676
Kennesaw State College 770.423.6151
Piedmont College 404.778.3000
Reinhardt College 770.720.5600
Savannah State College 912.356.2248
State University of Georgia 770.836.6516
Toccoa Falls College 404.886.6831
Truett-McConnell College 706.865.2134
University of Georgia 404.542.3737
Valdosta State College 912.333.5804
Waycross College 912.285.6135
West Georgia College 770.836.6516

HAWAII

Colleges & Universities
University of Hawaii-Honolulu 808.956.7756

IDAHO

Colleges & Universities
Albertson College of Idaho 208.459.5227
Boise State University 208.385.1771
Idaho State University 208.236.3636
North Idaho College 208.769.3300
Ricks College 208.356.1260
University of Idaho 208.885.6231

Private Instruction

Pat Flaherty's Drums & Percussion
2325 S. Five Mile Road Boise, ID 83709
P: 208.322.7419 **Playing:** 21 yrs all styles.
Teaching: 21 yrs drumset, hand perc, concert
& marching perc. / classical, jazz, rock, latin.
Level: All
Performer, symphony, jazz, top 40, d&b corps.
post graduate, masters & b.a. in music and
music education. teacher & conductor at various
colleges & univ. throughout U.S.

EDUCATION

Colleges & Universities

American Conservatory of Music	.312.263.4161
Augustana College	.309.794.7233
Belleville Area College	.618.235.2700
Benedictine University	.630.829.6320
Bradley University	.309.677.2595
Chicago Musical College	.312.341.3780
Chicago State University	.312.995.2155
College of Lake County	.312.223.6601
Concordia University	.708.209.3060
De Paul University	.312.325.7260
Eastern Illinois Univ.	.217.581.3010
Elmhurst College	.708.617.3515
Governors State Univ.	.708.534.5000
Illinois College	.217.245.3470
Illinois State Univ.	.309.438.7631
Illinois Wesleyan Univ.	.309.556.3061
Knox College	.309.341.7301
Lake Forest College	.847.735.5169
Lewis & Clark Comm. College	.618.467.2233
Lewis University	.815.838.0500
Lincoln Land Comm. College	.217.786.2320
Millikin University	.217.424.6300
Morton College	.708.656.8000
North Central College	.708.420.3432
Northern Illinois Univ.	.815.753.1551
Northwestern Univ.	.708.491.7575
Quincy University	.217.222.8020
Sherwood Conservatory	.312.427.6267
South Suburban College	.708.596.2000
Southern Ill. Univ.-Carbondale	.618.536.8742
Trinity College	.708.948.8980
Triton College	.708.456.0300
Univ. Of Illinois	.217.333.2620
Univ. of Illinois at Chicago	.319.996.2977
Vandercook College of Music	.312.225.6288
Western Illinois Univ.	.309.298.1544
Wheaton College	.708.752.5098

EDUCATION

William Rainey Harper College 708.397.3000

Private Instruction

Jeff Decker
255 E. Crest Ave. Bensenville, IL 60106
P: 630.595.2756
Playing: 27 yrs all styles.
Teaching: 19 yrs drumset / jazz, rock, latin.
Level: advanced
Tailor lessons to students needs.

INDIANA

Colleges & Universities

Anderson University 317.641.4450

Ball State University 317.285.5400

Butler University 317.940.9231

De Pauw University 317.658.4380
Earlham College 317.983.1200

Grace College 219.372.5280

Huntington College 219.356.6000

Indiana State Univ. 812.237.2771

Indiana Univ.-Bloomington 812.855.1582

Indiana Univ.-Purdue Univ. 219.481.6714

Indiana Univ. Southeast 812.941.2555

Indiana Univ.-South Bend 219.237.4134

Indiana Wesleyan Univ. 317.677.2152

Marian College 317.929.0302

Purdue University 317.494.0770

Saint Josephs College 219.866.6205

Taylor Univ.-Fort Wayne 219.456.7015

University of Evansville 812.479.2754

Univ. of Indianapolis 317.788.3255

Valparaiso Univ. 219.464.5454

Vincennes Univ. 812.885.4318

Wabash College 317.361.6473

EDUCATION

IOWA

Colleges & Universities
Buena Vista University 712.749.2131
Coe College 319.399.8521
Cornell College 319.895.4228
Dordt College 712.722.3771
Drake University 515.271.3975
Grinnell College 515.269.3064
Iowa State University 515.294.5364
Luther College 319.387.1208
North Iowa Area Comm.College ...515.421.4241
Northwestern College 712.737.7066
Southeastern Comm. College 319.752.2731
Southwestern Comm. College 515.782.7081
University of Iowa 319.335.1603
University of Northern Iowa 319.273.2024
Wartburg College 319.352.8214

KANSAS

Colleges & Universities
Baker University 913.594.6451
Bethany College 913.227.3311
Bethel College 316.284.5281
Central College 316.241.0723
Emporia State Univ. 316.341.5431
Fort Hays State Univ. 913.628.4226
Hutchinson Comm. Jr. College 316.665.3500
Kansas State University 913.532.5740
Labette Comm. College 316.421.3897
McPherson College 316.241.0731
Sterling College 316.278.2173
University of Kansas 913.864.3436
Washburn University 913.231.1010
Wichita State Univ. 316.689.3500

Schools
Professional Drum School 316.663.4004

EDUCATION

KENTUCKY

Colleges & Universities

Asbury College 606.858.3511
Bellarmine College 502.452.8224
Cumberland College 606.539.4332
Eaastern Kentucky Univ. 606.623.3266
Georgetown College 502.863.8100
Kentucky State University 502.227.6496
Morehead State Univ. 606.783.2473
Murray State University 502.762.6339
Northern Kentucky Univ. 606.572.6399
Transylvania University 606.233.8141

University of Kentucky- Lexington
105 Fine Arts Bldg. Lexington KY 40506-0022
P: 606.257.8181 **F:** 606.257.4104
Programs: BA, MA, DMA
Areas: Total percussion, all styles
Faculty: James Campbell

University of Louisville 502.852.6907
Western Kentucky Univ. 502.745.3751

LOUISIANA

Colleges & Universities

Centenary College of Louisiana . . .318.869.5235
Grambling State Univ. 318.274.2682
Louisiana State Univ. 504.388.3261
Louisiana Tech Univ. 318.257.4223
Loyola University 504.865.3037
Northeast Louisiana Univ. 318.342.1570
Northwest State Univ. of LA 318.357.4522
Southern University 504.771.3440
Tulane Univ. of Louisiana 504.865.5267
Univ. of Southwestern Louisiana . .318.482.6016
University of New Orleans 504.286.6381
Xavier Univ. of Louisiana 504.483.7621

EDUCATION

MAINE

Colleges & Universities

Bates College	.207.786.6137
Univ. of Maine-Augusta	.207.621.3274
Univ. of Maine-Machias	.207.255.3314
Univ. of Maine-Orono	.207.581.4700
Univ. of Southern Maine	.207.780.5265

MARYLAND

Colleges & Universities

Catonsville Comm. College	.410.455.4109
Columbia Union College	.301.270.9200
Essex Community College	.410.780.6521
Frederick Comm. College	.301.846.2512
Frostburg State University	.301.689.4109
Garrett Community College	.301.387.3000
Goucher College	.301.337.6276
Hagerstown Junior College	.301.790.2800
Harford Community College	.410.836.4291
Montgomery College	.301.279.5209
Morgan State University	.301.319.3286
Mount Saint Marys College	.301.447.5308
Peabody Conservatory of Music	.410.659.8150
Western Maryland College	.410.857.2595

MASSACHUSSETTS

Colleges & Universities

Anna Maria College	.508.849.3450
Berklee College of Music	.617.266.1400
Boston Conservatory	.617.536.6340
Boston University	.617.353.3341
Bridgewater State College	.508.697.1377
Clark University	.508.793.7340
Dean College	.508.528.9100

EDUCATION

MASSACHUSSETTS

Eastern Nazarene College	.617.773.6350
Gordon College	.508.927.2300
Holyoke Comm. College	.413.538.7000
New England Conservatory	.617.262.1120
Tufts University	.617.627.3564
Univ. of Massachusetts-Amherst	.413.545.4313
Univ. of Massachusetts-Boston	.617.287.6980
Univ. of Massachusetts-Dartmouth	.508.999.8568
Univ. of Massachusetts-Lowell	.508.934.3850
Westfield State College	.413.568.3311

Private Instruction
Yvonne L. Wollak
288 South Street Ext. Medfield, MA 02052
P: 508.359.7239 **Teaching:** 19 yrs drumset, concert & marching perc., mallets / jazz, rock, latin, big band, funk. **Level:** all
B.S. degree in music education. Former student of Alan Dawson, Bob Varney. Performer (drums/ vocals) & studio drummer, freelance.

MICHIGAN

Colleges & Universities

Adrian College	.517.265.5161
Albion College	.517.629.0467
Alma College	.517.463.7161
Aquinas College	.616.459.8281
Calvin College	.616.957.6253
Central Michigan Univ.	.517.774.3281
Cornerstone College	.616.285.1522
Eastern Michigan Univ.	.313.487.0244
Grand Valley State Univ.	.616.895.3484
Hillsdale College	.517.437.7341
Hope College	.616.395.7650
Kalamazoo College	.616.337.7070
Lake Michigan College	.616.927.8100
Michigan State Univ.	.517.355.4583
Northwestern Michigan College	.616.922.1338
Oakland University	.810.370.2030

EDUCATION

Siena Heights College 517.263.0731
Spring Arbor College 517.750.1200
Univ. of Michigan-Ann Harbor 313.764.0583
Wayne State University 313.577.1795

Private Instruction

Dave Tranquilla
601 Axtell Kalamazoo, MI 49008
P/F: 616.342.1636 **Playing:** 12 yrs all styles.
Teaching: 5 yrs drumset, hand percussion / jazz,
rock, latin, funk, big band, country. **Level:** all.
Wide array of exp. including many sub gigs, studio
work & improvisational playing.

MINNESOTA

Colleges & Universities

Augsburg College 816.942.8400
Bemidji State University 218.755.2915
Bethel College 612.638.6400
Carleton College 507.663.4347
College of Saint Benedict 612.363.5684
Concordia College 218.299.4414
Gustavas Adolphus College 507.933.7364
Hamline University 612.641.2438
Macalester College 612.696.6382
Mankato State University 507.389.2118
Miineapolis Comm. College 612.341.7307
Moorehead State Univ. 216.236.2101
Northwest College. 612.631.5218
St. Mary's Coll. of Minnesota 507.452.4430
Saint Olaf College 507.646.3180
Southwest State Univ. 507.537.7234
St. Cloud State Univ. 612.255.3223
University of Minnesota-Duluth 218.281.8266
Univ. of Minn.-Minneapolis 612.624.5093
Univ. of Minn.-Morris 612.589.2211
Univ. of Saint Thomas 612.962.5850
Vermilion Comm. College. 218.365.3256

Schools

Music Tech 612.338.0175

EDUCATION

MISSISSIPPI

Colleges & Universities

Delta State University 601.846.4615
Hinds Comm. College 601.857.3271
Jackson State University 601.968.2141
Jones County Jr. College 601.477.4094
Mississippi College 601.925.3440
Mississippi Gulf Coast Coll. 601.928.6211
Mississippi State Univ. 601.325.3070
Mississippi Valley State Univ. 601.254.3482
N.E. Mississippi Comm. Coll. 601.728.7751
Pearl River Comm. College 601.795.6801
Univ. of Mississippi 601.232.7268
Univ. of Southern Mississippi 601.266.5363

MISSOURI

Colleges & Universities

Central Methodist College 816.248.3391
Central Missouri State Univ. 816.543.4530
Drury College 417.873.7296
Evangel College 417.865.2811
Lindenwood College 314.949.4906
Missouri Western State College . . .816.271.4420
N.E. Missouri State Univ. 816.785.4417
N.W. Missouri State Univ. 816.562.1315
Saint Louis University 314.658.2410
S.E. Missouri State Univ. 314.651.2141
Southwest Baptist University 417.326.1630
S.W. Missouri State Univ. 417.836.5648
Three Rivers Comm. College 314.840.9639
Univ. of Missouri-Columbia 314.882.2604
Univ. of Missouri-Kansas City 816.235.2900
Washington University 314.935.5581
Webster University 314.968.6900
William Jewell College 816.781.7700

EDUCATION

MONTANA

Colleges & Universities

Montana State Univ.-Billings 406.657.2350
Rocky Mountain College 406.657.1000

NEBRASKA

Colleges & Universities

Central Comm. College-Platte. 402.564.7132
Chadron State College 308.432.6000
Dana College 402.426.7310
Hastings College 402.463.2402
Nebraska Wesleyan Univ. 402.465.2269
Peeru State College 402.872.2237
Univ. of Nebraska-Kearney 308.865.8618
Univ. of Nebraska-Lincoln 402.472.2503
Univ. of Nebraska-Omaha 402.554.2251
Wayne State College 402.375.7359

NEVADA

Colleges & Universities

Univ. of Nevada-Las Vegas 702.895.4195

NEW HAMPSHIRE

Colleges & Universities

Dartmouth College 603.646.2530
Franklin Pierce College 603.899.4206
Keene State College 603.358.2177
Plymouth State College 603.535.2334
Univ. of New Hampshire 603.862.2404

Call us to have your name or school here next year 718.875.6353

EDUCATION

NEW JERSEY

Colleges & Universities

Jersey City State College 201.200.3151
Montclair State University 201.655.7212
Rowan Coll. of New Jersey 609.256.4555
Rutgers State Univ.-Camden 609.757.6209
Rutgers State Univ.-New Brnswk . .908.932.9302
Rutgers State Univ.-Newark 201.648.5119
Seton Hall University 201.761.9459
Trenton State College 609.771.2551
Upsala College 201.266.7281

Private Instruction

Ray's Drum Studio
52 Mountain Trail Branchville, NJ 07826
P/F: 201.948.0729 **Eml:** rtreg@palace.net.
Playing: 20 yrs rock, funk, blues.
Teaching: drumset / beginner music theory, time
development. **Level:** Beginner & intermediate.
Call Ray Tregellas.

Russ Moy
2165 Morris Ave. Union NJ 07083
P: 908.686.7736
Playing: 46 yrs **Teaching:** 35 yrs all styles
Individual instruction on drumset, hand percussion,
including djembe timbales, conga, bongos, +
reading / rock, jazz, big band, Latin, show, &
fusion, in contemporary & ethnic styles. **Levels:** All
Study with one of the most knowledgable &
sincere pros in the business. Call for appt.
Also available for "Drums Drums Drums" school
program.

NEW MEXICO

Colleges & Universities

Eastern New Mexico Univ. 505.562.2376
San Juan CollegeNM 505.326.3311
University of New Mexico 505.277.2126
Webster New Mexico Univ. 505.538.6614

EDUCATION

NEW YORK

Colleges & Universities

Adelphi University	516.877.4290
Binghamton Univ.-SUNY	607.777.2591
Brooklyn College-CUNY	718.951.5286
City Univ. of NY-Grad Ctr.	212.642.2301
College at Fredonia-SUNY	716.673.3151
College at Geneseo-SUNY	716.245.5824
College Of Saint Rose	518.454.5178
Concordia College	914.337.9300
Daemen College	716.839.8265
Finger Lakes Comm. Coll.	716.394.3500
Hamilton College	315.859.4350
Hobart & Williams Smith Coll.	315.781.3401
Hofstra University	516.463.5490
Houghton College	716.567.9400
Ithaca College	607.274.3171
Jamstown Comm. College	716.665.5220
Julliard School	212.799.5000
Manhattan School of Music	212.749.2802
Manhattanville College	914.694.2200
Mannes College of Music	212.580.0210
Mercy College	914.693.4500
Nassau Community College	516.222.7447
Nazareth College	716.586.2525
New York University	212.998.5424
Onandaga Comm. College	315.469.2256
Purchase College-SUNY	914.251.6700
Queens College-CUNY	718.997.3800
Queensborough Comm. Coll.	718.631.6393
Robert's Wesleyan Univ.	716.594.9471
Schenectady Cty Comm. Coll.	518.346.6211
Skidmore College	518.584.5000
State Univ. of NY-Albany	518.442.4187
State Univ. of NY-Buffalo	716.636.2765
State Univ. of NY-New Paltz	914.257.2700

EDUCATION

State Univ. of NY-Stony Brook 516.632.7330

Staten Island College-CUNY 718.982.2520

SUNY-College at Potsdam 315.267.2415

Syracuse University 315.443.2191

Ulster Community College 914.687.5060

Vassar College 914.437.7319

Villa Maria Coll. of Buffalo 716.896.0700

Wagner College 718.390.3313

Westchester Consrv of Music 914.761.3715

Schools

Boys Harbor Perf. Arts Ctr. 212.427.2244

Drummer's Collective
541 Ave of the Americas, NYC, NY 10011
P: 212.741.0091 **F:** 212 604.0760
Eml: DC@thecoll.com
Programs: 10 wk certificate, 6 wk adv. certificate,
4wk certificate prep, & five day intensive.
Setting: group, individual.
Disciplines: drumset, hand perc / jazz, rock,
latin, contemporary & ethnic styles."

School of Musical Performance
910 Kings Hwy Brooklyn, NY 11223
P/F: 718.339.4989
Programs: non -degree. **Setting:** Individual
Disciplines: drumset, vibraphone, marimba /
classical, jazz, rock, latin, big band, charts/ jazz
improv. Author "Vibraphone Virtuosity" &
Vibraphonie Portfolio".

Private Instruction

Edmund C. Dicapua
P.O. Box 893 East Quogue, NY 11942
P: 516.723.0214
Playing: 30 yrs w/ jazz, rock groups, chamber &
symp. orch, shows. **Teaching:** 20 yrs drumset,
hand perc., concert & marching perc. / classical,
jazz, rock, Latin. **Level:** All.   Make house calls.

Private Instruction cont'd

Female Drummer's Workshop, NYC
832 Metropolitan Ave. Bklyn, NY 11211
P: 718.486.8147 **Playing:** 15 yrs all styles.
Teaching: 12 yrs drumset / rock, blues, funk, marching. **Level:** All
Focus caters to the student needs of female drumset players. all levels, beginners encouraged.

Tim Heckman
25-47 12th Street, Astoria NY 11102
P: 718.545.5895
Playing: 7 yrs Classical **Teaching:** 7 yrs Concert & Marching percussion. Specializing in Marimba. **Level:** All
Also expand tech. capabilities, play faxter & stronger with Feldenkrais- awareness through movement lessons begining Spring 98.

Norman Hedman
484 West 43 St., NYC NY 10036
P: 212.736.0585 **F:** 212.594.5428
Playing: 30 yrs African, r&b, pop, Latin
Teaching: 7 yrs hand percussion/ African, Latin, world music jazz, funk **Levels:** All
Also teaches at Drummers Collective. Has perf. w/ Nancy Wilson, Arturo Sandoval, Chico Freeman, Von Freeman, The Jacksons, Hall & Oats, Earth, Wind & Fire, Branford Marsalis to name a few.

Mario Monaco
N.Y.C. **P:** 718.274.9809
Playing & Teaching: 30 yrs
Disciplines: drumset & Brazilian percussion. Specializing in pandeiro, berimbau, timba, rebo-lo, reco-reco, tamborim, sourdo, zabumba & repenique. **Levels:** All

See ad on opposite page.

John Sarracco
187 Locust Ave. Staten Island, NY 10306
P: 718.351.4031
NYC Drummers: Study with John Sarracco, one of the most knowledgeable pros in the NY area. Accepting only the serious-minded for drum instruction the professional way. Manhattan and Staten Island studio locations.

EDUCATION

NORTH CAROLINA

Colleges & Universities

Appalachian State Univ. 704.262.3020
Barton College 919.399.6300
Brevard College 704.883.8292
Campbell University 919.893.4111
Davidson College 704.892.2357
Duke University 919.660.3300
East Carolina University 919.328.6851
Elizabeth City State Univ. 919.335.3359
Elon College 919.584.2440
Gardner Webb Univ. 704.434.4448
Greensboro College 919.272.7102
Lenoir Rhyne College 704.328.7147
Mars Hill College 704.689.1209
Meredith College 919.829.8536
N. Carolina A&T State Univ. 910.334.7926
N. Carolina School of the Arts 919.770.3399
N. Carolina State Univ. 919.515.2981
Pembroke State Univ. 910.521.6230
Pfeiffer College 704.463.1360
Sacred Heart College 704.825.5146
Saint Augustine's College 919.828.4451
Univ. of N. Carolina-Asheville 704.251.6432
Univ. of N. Carolina-Chapel Hill . . .919.962.3320
Univ. of N. Carolina-Charlotte 704.547.2472
Univ. of N.Carolina-Greensboro . . .910.334.5789
Wake Forest University 910.759.5346
Western Carolina Univ. 704.227.7242
Wingate University 704.233.8038

NORTH DAKOTA

Colleges & Universities

Minot State University 701.857.3185
N. Dakota State University 701.231.7932
University of Mary 701.255.7500
Univ. of N. Dakota -Grand Forks . . .701.777.2644
Valley City State Univ. 701.845.7272

EDUCATION

OHIO

Colleges & Universities

Baldwin - Wallace College 216.826.2362
Bluffton College 419.358.3000
Bowling Green State Univ. 419.372.2181
Capital University 614.236.6474
Central State University 513.376.6403
Cleveland Institute of Music 216.791.5000
Cleveland State University 216.687.2033
College of Wooster 216.263.2419
Cuyahoga Comm. Coll. West 216.987.5508
East Central University 405.332.800x390
Hiram College 216.569.5294
Kent State University 216.672.2172
Kenyon College 614.427.5197
Malone College 216.471.8231
Miami College 513.529.3014
Mount. St. Joseph College 513.244.4863
Mount Union College 216.823.2180
Muskingum College 614.826.8182
Ohio Northern Univ. 419.772.2151
Ohio State University 614.292.6571
Ohio University 614.593.4244
Ohio Wesleyan University 614.368.3700
University of Akron 216.972.7590
University of Cincinnati 513.556.3737
University of Dayton 513.229.3936
University of Findlay 419.422.8313
Wittenberg College 513.327.7341
Wright State University 513.873.2346
Xavier Universtiy 513.745.3801

OKLAHOMA

Colleges & Universities

Cameron Universtiy 405.581.2440
Oklahoma Christian Univ. 405.425.5530
Oklahoma City University 405.521.5316
Oklahoma Panhandle State Univ. . .405.349.2611

EDUCATION

Phillips University 405.237.4433x200
SW Oklahoma State Univ. 405.774.3708
Univ. of Central Oklahoma . .405.341.2980x5004
University of Oklahoma 405.325.2081
University of Tulsa 918.631.2262
Western Oklahoma State College . .405.477.2000

OREGON

Colleges & Universities

Eastern Oregon State Coll. 503.962.3629
Lewis & Clark College 503.768.7460
Linfield College 503.434.2275
Pacific University 503.359.2216
Portland State Univ. 503.725.3011
Southern Oregon State Coll. 503.552.6101
Southwestern Oregon State Coll. .503.888.2525x249
Umpqua Comm. College 503.440.4693
University of Oregon 503.346.3761
University of Portland 503.283.7228
Warner Pacific College 503.775.4366x711
Western Oregon State Coll. 503.838.8275
Willamette University 503.370.6255

PENNSYLVANIA

Colleges & Universities

Allegheny College 814.332.3356
Bloomsburg University 717.389.4284
Bucks County Comm. Coll. 215.968.8088
Carnegie Mellon Univ. 412.268.2385
Chatham College 412.365.1205
Clarion University of Penn. 814.226.2287
Curtis Institute of Music 215.893.5252

EDUCATION

Drexel University 215.895.2452
Duquesne University 412.396.6080
Edinboro Univ. Of Penn. 814.732.2555
Elizabethtown College 717.361.1212
Geneva College 412.847.6660
Gettysburg College 717.337.6131
Immaculata College 610.647.4400
Indiana Univ. of Pennsylvania 412.357.2390
Juniata College 814.641.3473
Kutztown Universtiy 215.683.4550
Lafayette College 215.250.5356
Lebanon Valley College 717.867.6275
Lehigh Universtiy 610.758.3835
Lock Haven University 717.893.2127
Lycoming College 717.321.4016
Mansfield University 717.662.4710
Mercyhurst College 814.824.2394
Messiah College 717.766.2511
Moravian College 610.861.1650
Muhlenberg College 610.821.3363
Penn State Univ. - Univ. Park 814.865.0431
Seton Hill College 412.834.2200
Slippery Rock University 412.738.2063
Temple University 215.204.8301
University of the Arts 215.875.2206
West Chester University 610.436.2739
Westminster College 412.946.7270
Wilkes University 717.831.4420

Private Instruction

Edgar Bateman Jr.
401 Washington Ave. # 2003 Philadelphia, PA 19147
P: 215.463.6070
Playing: 40 yrs jazz, gospel, r&b, soul, etc.
Teaching: 20 yrs drumset, snare / jazz, rudiments. **Level:** All.
Recording, performing exp. w/many major artists.

EDUCATION

RHODE ISLAND

Colleges & Universities

Salve Regina University 401.847.6650x2945
Univ. Of Rhode Island 401.792.2431

SOUTH CAROLINA

Colleges & Universities

Anderson College 803.231.2125
Bob Jones Universtiy 803.242.5100x2712
Charleston Southern Univ. 803.863.7972
Clemson University 864.656.3043
Coastal Carolina Univ. 803.347.3161x2513
Furman University 864.294.2086
Lander University 803.229.8323
Limestone College 864.488.4508
Newberry College 803.321.5174
Nth Greenville College 803.895.1410
Univ. of Sth Carolina- Colombia . . .803.777.4280
Winthrop University 803.323.2255

SOUTH DAKOTA

Colleges & Universities

Augustana College 605.336.5451
South Dakota State Univ. 605.688.5187
Univ. of Souix Falls 605.331.6637
Univ. of South Dakota 605.677.5274

TENNESSEE

Colleges & Universities

Austin Peay State Univ. 615.648.7818
Belmont University 615.385.6408
Carson- Newman College 615.471.3328

EDUCATION

Dyersberg State Comm .Coll. 901.285.6910

East Tennessee State Univ. 615.929.4270

Maryville College 423.981.8150

Middle Tennessee State Univ. 615.898.2469

Rhodes College 901.726.3775

Shelby State Comm. College 901.528.6841

Tennessee State Univ. 615.320.3544

Tennessee Tech University 615.372.3161

Union University 901.668.1818

University of Memphis 901.678.2541

Univ. of Tennessee- Chatanooga . .423.755.4601

Univ. of Tennessee-Knoxville 423.974.3241

Univ. Of Tennessee- Martin 901.587.7402

Vanderbilt University 615.322.7651

Private Instruction

Lindenwood Studio of Percussion
2400 Union Ave. Memphis, TN 38112
P: 901.458.8506 **F:** 901.458.8509 x36
Playing: 23 yrs classical, rock, jazz **Teaching:** 20 yrs
Drumset, concert & marching perc., mallet ensemble / classical, jazz, rock, latin.
Level: All
Stan Head- timpanist w/ Jackson Symphony
Orch.. X-tra perc. for Memphis Symphony Orch.

TEXAS

Colleges & Universities

Abiline Christian Univ. 915.674.2199

Alvin Comm. College 713.388.4792

Amarillo College 806.371.5340

Angelo State University 915.942.2085

Baylor University 817.755.1161

Blinn College 409.830.4261

Cedar Valley College-Dallas 214.372.8120

Cisco Jr. College 817.442.2567

Dallas County Comm College 214.333.8632

EDUCATION

Del Mar College 512.886.1211

East Texas Baptist Univ. 903.935.7963

Houston Baptist Univ. 713.995.3338

Howard Payne Univ. 915.649.8500

Kilgore College 903.984.8531

Lamar University 409.880.8144

Mclennan Comm. College 817.750.3483

McMurry University 915.691.6391

Midwestern State Univ. 817.689.4267

Navarro College 903.874.6501

Prairie View A&M Univ. 409.857.3919

Rice University 713.527.4854

Saint Mary's University 512.436.3421

Sam Houston State Univ. 409.294.1360

San Antonio College 512.733.2731

San Jacinto College Central 713.476.1830

San Jacinto College North 713.458.4050

San Jacinto College South 713.484.1900

South Plains College 806.894.9661x275

Southern Methodist Univ. 214.768.2643

Southwest Texas State Univ. 512.245.2651

Southwestern Adventist College . . .817.645.3921

Tarleton State Univ. 817.968.9245

Temple College 817.773.9961x300

Texas A&M Univ.- Commerce 903.886.5303

Texas A&M Univ.- Corpus Christie . . .512.994.2314

Texas A&M Univ.- Kingsville 512.593.2803

Texas Christian Univ. 817.921.7602

Texas Southern Univ. 713.527.7337

Texas Tech University 806.742.2270

Trinity University 210.736.8212

Trinity Valley Comm. College 214.675.6238

Tyler Jr. College 903.510.2483

Univ. of Houstion 713.743.3009

Univ. of North Texas 817.565.2791

Univ. of Texas - Arlington 817.272.3471

Univ. of Texas - Austin 512.471.7764

Univ. of Texas - Brownsville 210.544.8247

EDUCATION

TEXAS cont'd

Univ. of Texas - El Paso 915.747.5606
Univ. of Texas - San Antonio 210.458.4355
University of Houston 713.743.3009
West Texas A&M Univ. 806.656.2840
Wharton County Jr. College 713.532.6365

UTAH

Colleges & Universities
Bringham Young Univ. 801.378.3083
Southern Utah Univ. 801.586.7890
University of Utah 801.581.6765
Weber State University 801.626.6437

VERMONT

Colleges & Universities
Bennington College 802.442.5401
Johnson State College 802.635.2356x310
University of Vermont 802.656.3040

VIRGINIA

Colleges & Universities
Bridgewater College 703.828.2501
College of William & Mary 804.221.1071
George Mason University 703.993.1380
Jame Madison University 540.568.6197
Longwood College 804.395.2504
Mary Washington College 540.654.1012
Norfolk State College 804.683.8544
Old Dominion College 804.683.4061
Radford University 703.831.5177
University of Richmond 804.289.8277
VA Polytech Inst & State Univ. 703.231.5685
Virginia Commonwealth Univ. 804.828.1166

EDUCATION

WASHINGTON

Colleges & Universities

Central Washington Univ. 509.963.1216
Cornish College of the Arts 206.726.5030
Eastern Washington Univ. 509.359.2241
Gonzaga University 509.328.4220x3333
Grays Harbor College 206.532.9020
Pacific Lutheran Univ. 206.535.7601
Peninsula College 360.452.9277x6437
Pierce College 206.964.6220
Seattle Pacific Univ. 206.281.2205
Spokane Falls Comm. College 509.533.3720
Univ. of Washington 206.543.1201
Walla Walla College 509.527.2561
Western Washington Univ. 206.650.3130
Washington State University 509.335.8524

Private Instruction

John Bishop
5206 1/2 Ballard Ave. NW #11 Seattle, WA 98107
P: 206.781.2589 **Eml:** johnbishop@msn.com
Web: teleport.com/~tperfect/ns/newStories.htm1
Playing: 29 yrs all styles, mostly jazz.
Teaching: 20 yrs drumset / technique, concepts,
phrasing, perspective. all styles.
Level: intermediate & advance. Active profes-
sional, recording and touring with various major
artists, film scores, jingles, 20+ cd's.

WEST VIRGINIA

Colleges & Universities

Glenville State College 304.462.7361
Marshall University 304.696.3117
Potomac St. Coll of West VA 304.788.6959
Shepard College 304.876.5225
W. Liberty State College 304.336.8006
W. Virginia State College 304.766.3196
W. Virginia Univ. Morgantown 304.293.4617

EDUCATION

WISCONSIN

Colleges & Universities

Alverno College 414.382.6137

Beloit College 608.363.2372

Concordia Univ. Wisconsin 414.243.5700

Lawrence University 414.832.6611

Milwaukee Area Tech College 414.278.6778

Northland College 715.682.1304

Silver Lake College 414.684.6691x172

Univ. of Wisconsin- Barron Cty 715.234.8176

Univ. of Wisconsin- Eau Claire 715.836.2284

Univ. of Wisconsin- Green Bay 414.465.2348

Univ. of Wisconsin- Madison 608.263.1900

Univ. of Wisconsin- Milwaukee 414.229.4393

Univ. of Wisconsin- Oshkosh 414.424.4224

Univ. of Wisconsin- Parkside 414.595.2547

Univ. of Wisconsin- River Falls 715.425.3183

Univ. of Wisconsin- Steven Pt. 715.346.3107

Univ. of Wisconsin- Superior 715.394.8115

Univ. of Wisconsin- Whitewater 414.472.1310

Wisconsin Consv. of Music, WI 414.276.5760

Private Instruction

Drum Instructors Guild
7920 St. Anne Ct. Wauwatosa (Milwk) WI 53213
P: 414.774.1462 **F:** 414.774.4919
Programs: Drum Set Qwik Start, Drum Line
Coaching, Hand Drum Intensives.
Settings: Individual & Group.
Disciplines: drumset, hand drums, concert &
marching perc / Jazz, rock, classical, ethnic,
marching.
Levels: Beginner to advanced.12 locations & in
home.

WYOMING

Colleges & Universities

Casper College 307.268.2606

Northwest College 307.754.6301

University of Wyoming 307.766.5242

CANADA

Universities & Colleges
Alberta

Alberta College 403.425.7401

Grande Prairie Regional College . . 403.539.2909

Grant Macewan Comm. College . . 403.483.2312

Medicine Hat College 403.529.3880

Mount Royal College 403.240.6821

Prairie Bible College 403.443.5511

University of Calgary 403.220.5376

University of Lethbridge 403.329.2338

British Columbia

Selkirk College 604.354.3257

Trinity Western University 604.888.7511

University of British Columbia 604.822.3113

Vancouver Academy of Music 604.734.2301

Manitoba

Brandon University 204.727.9631

Nova Scotia

St. Francis Xavier University 902.867.2106

Ontario

Huntington College 705.673.4126

McMaster University 905.525.9140

Royal Conservatory of Music 416.408.2824

University of Toronto 416.978.3750

University of Western Ontario 519.661.2043

Quebec

McGill University 514.398.4535

Universite Laval 418.656.7061

University de Montreal 514.343.6429

School

Bannf Ctr for Perf. Arts 800.565.9989

CARIBBEAN

Colleges & Universities
Puerto Rico

Interamerican University 809.892.1095
Puerto Rico Consrv. of Music 809.751.0160
Universidad de Puerto Rico 809.764.0000x2293

EUROPE

England

Drumatic Drum Tuition
Carshalton 44.181.669.3514

Drumtech . . . . .London 44.181.749.3131

Musicians Institute - London
London 44.171.265.0284

Orchard Percussion Studio
Colchester 44.120. 627.1634

Soner & Hohner Drum School
Surbiton, ...44.181.399.1166

France

Drum School . . . . .Toulouse   61.80.12.41
École de BatterieDante AgostiniLille 20.51.18.03
Objectif Musik . . . . .Ivry Sur Seine   46.71.34.00
Tama/ Paiste Drums Schools
Cedex 33.1.39.93.26.88

Germany

Drummers Focus . . . . .Munich   49.89.273.1091
Drummers Focus . . . .Stuttgart 49.711.234.9933
Drummers Institute .Dusseldorf 49.211.790.0574

Italy

Timba-Scuola di Batteria e Perc
Rome 06.556.6099
Universita Della Musica
Rome .39.6.574.7885
Drummers Initiative\
Amsterdam 31.20.675.7150
Drumschool Cleuver
Den Haag 31.70.355.0647

Switzerland

Acad. of Contemp. Music . . . .Zurich 41.1.252.2030
Drumschool + Perc. Shop. . . .Basel .41.61.271.7487

MIXED MEDIA

BOOKS

Publishers

Alfred Publishing 800.625.3733
Amatucci Productions 707.445.4626

Barrel of Monkeys Publishing
1573 Cross Way San Jose, CA 95125
P: 888.971.7179 **F:** 408.998.5470
Eml: CCooper@aol
Web: http://www.musicdata.com/chopsbusters
Chop Busters, the only modern drum book
devoted to technique. exercises, patterns, rudi-
ments & rolls. Also "Solo Music for Snare Drum".
See Coupon Section for $avings.

Bradley Music Co. 818 881.2258
C. Alan Publications 910.665.6116
Cydar Publishing 520.751-0767
Drumworks Publishing 800.431.1358
Galerie Amrad African Art Publ. . . 514.931.4747
Garland Publishing 800.627.6273
J.R. Publications 305.563.1844
JB Publications 618 277.3864
Ken Cox Publishing 800.520.8888
Meredith Music Publ. 954.563.9006
Percussive Arts Society 405.353.1455
RMI Music Productions 954.345.6551
Smith Publications 410.298.6509
The Modern Drummer Library 800.637.2852
Warner Bros. Music Publ. 305 620.1500
White Cliffs Media, Inc. 603.357.0236

Sources

Books Now 800.962.6651x8500

Drummers Corner - David Hunt
PO Box 4397, West Hills CA 91308-4397
P: 800:425.0427 F: 818.704.3918
Web: drummers corner.com
Online resource dedicated to helping you find
whatever you need in books & videos to take you
to the next level.

Drum Charts Int'l 914.6.charts
Nat'l Drum Assoc.(NDA) 212.768.3768
Percussion Express 815.229.3131
Steve Weiss Music 215.329.1639
World Music Institute 212.545.7536

MIXED MEDIA

MUSIC SOURCES

Concert/Keyboard Percussion
HoneyRock 814.652.6886

Drumset / Drummers
Audiophile Imports 410.628.7601

World Music

Australian
Australian Music Int'l 212.253.1567

Celtic
Living Music Records 860.567.8796
Maggies Music 410.268.3395

Latin American
Bembe Records 707.923.7262
Descarga 718.693.2966
Qualiton Imports 718.937.8515

Native American
Canyon Records Prod. 800.268.1141
Sound of America Records 505.268.6110

General
Chesky Records 800.331.1437

Ethos Percussion Group
PO Box 397 East Elmhurst NY 11369
P&F: 718.661.3334
Eml: ethos@earthlink.net
Web: http://home.earthlink.net/~
CD's available: Ethos Perc Group Debut $13,
Bizet/Shchedrin Carmen Fantasy $15, Ethos &
Paramount Brass: Changing w/ the Times $10.
See Coupon section for $avings.

Interworld Music 802.257.5519
Intuition Music 800.473.1175
Irresistible Rhythms Inc. 800.969.5269
Moment Records 415.459.6994
Museline 617.497.lstn x7825
Music of the World 919.932.9600
Nimbus Records 800.326.0823
Redwood Records 800.888.7664
Smithsonian/ Folkways 800.410.9815
Steve Weiss Music 215.329.1639
Talking Drum Records 310.396.6941
Whirled Disc 415.454.4420
White Cliffs Media, Inc. 603.357.0236
World Music Distribution 800.900.4527
World Music Institute 212.545.7536

1. **GIOVANNI HIDALGO:** Conga Virtuoso ORDER TL-13827 $39.95

2. **GIOVANNI HIDALGO:** In The Tradition ORDER TL-15220 $39.95

3. **GIOVANNI HIDALGO:** One On One / Mano A Mano ORDER TL-15477 $39.95

4. **BOBBY SANABRIA:** Getting Started On Congas: Conga Basics ORDER TL-14924 $19.95

5. **BOBBY SANABRIA:** Fundamento 1 - Technique For 1 & 2 Drums ORDER TL-15064 $24.95

6. **BOBBY SANABRIA:** Fundamento 2 - Technique For 2 & 3 Drums ORDER TL-15065 $24.95

7. **CHANGUITO:** History Of The Songo ORDER TL-15221 $39.95

8. **CHANGUITO:** Evolution Of The Tumbadores ORDER TL-15476 $39.95

9. **GIOVANNI HIDALGO & CHANGUITO:** Conga Masters: Duets ORDER TL-14188 $19.95

10. **KIM ATKINSON:** Mozambique! ORDER TL-15640 $39.95

11. **SANTANA RHYTHM SECTION:** From Afro-Cuban To Rock ORDER TL-14507 $37.95

12. **MANNY OQUENDO:** Manny Oquendo On Timbales & Bongo ORDER TL-15359 $39.95

13. **GIOVANNI HIDALGO & CHANGUITO:** Conga Masters: The Masters Meet Again ORDER TL-15222 $19.95

14. **GIOVANNI HIDALGO & STEVE GADD:** 1997 Modern Drummer Festival ORDER TL-16204 $39.95

15. **IGNACIO BERROA:** Mastering The Art Of Afro-Cuban Drumming ORDER TL-13828 $39.95

16. **VARIOUS ARTISTS:** Drumset Artists Of Cuba ORDER TL-16074 $24.95

17. **LINCOLN GOINES & ROBBY AMEEN:** Afro-Cuban Grooves For Bass & Drums ORDER TL-11538 $39.95

18. **FRANCISCO AGUABELLA:** Sworn To The Drum: A Tribute To Francisco Aquabella TL-14764 $39.95

4
GETTING STARTED ON CONGAS
CONGA BASICS
BiLingual ENGLISH/ESPAÑOL
with Bobby Sanabria

5
GETTING STARTED ON CONGAS
TECHNIQUE FOR ONE AND TWO DRUMS
with Bobby Sanabria
BiLingual ENGLISH/ESPAÑOL
FUNDAMENTO 1 BOOKLET INCLUDED

6
GETTING STARTED ON CONGAS
TECHNIQUE FOR TWO AND THREE DRUMS
with Bobby Sanabria
Special Guest: Candido Camero
BiLingual ENGLISH/ESPAÑOL
FUNDAMENTO 2 BOOKLET INCLUDED

10
mozambique!
VOLUME I
TOP SECRET
with Kim Atkinson
(INTERMEDIATE/ADVANCED - CONGA)

11
FROM AFRO-CUBAN TO ROCK
ADVENTURES IN CULTURE

12
MANNY OQUENDO
On Timbales
(BONGO'S, COWBELLS, MARACAS, GUIRO)
ALCHEMY PICTURES

16
DRUMSET ARTISTS of Cuba

17
FUNKIFYING THE CLAVE
Afro-Cuban Grooves for Bass and Drums
LINCOLN GOINES AND ROBBY AMEEN
BiLingual ENGLISH/ESPAÑOL
Over 90 minutes with Six Tunes

18
Flower Films Presents
SWORN TO THE DRUM:
A Tribute to Francisco Aguabella
DIRECTED AND PHOTOGRAPHED BY LES BLANK
PRODUCED BY TOM LUDDY

MIXED MEDIA

VIDEOS

Producers

Cherry Lane Music, Co. 914 935.5200

Collected Edition/ TAP Prod. 404.873.5118

Dancing Hands Music 800.898.8036

DCI Music Videos 212.691.1884

Hot Licks Video 800.388.3008

Interworld Music 800.698.6705

Multicultural Media 800.550.9675

Music Video Products, Inc. 818.709.5809

Warner Bros. Music Publ. 305 620.1500

African & World Percussion Arts
115 S. Topanga Cyn. Blvd #169, Topanga CA 90290
P: 818.591.3111/ 800.733.Drum **F:** 818.591.6756
Eml: drum1@pacificnet.net **Web:** www.pacificnet/~drum1
Hands on drumming: Universal Keys to Hand
Drumming Vol. I-VI, djembe drumming, videos, cd's,
cassettes, the top rated, comprehensive series.

The Doumbeck Video
1812 Gillespie St., Santa Barbara CA 93101
P: 805.898.0663 **Eml:** kesslari@ix.netcom.com
Web:http://www.netcom.com/~kesslari/doumvid.html
The Ultimate Doumbek Instructional Video! Lets
you develop your skills on this amazing hand
drum while your learn the rhythms of the
mysterious Middle East.

Sources

Books Now 800.962.6651x8500

Descarga 718.693.2966

Drum Charts Int'l 914.6.Charts

Interworld Music 800.698.6705

Music Dispatch 800.637.2852

Music Mail Ltd. (Europe) 44.147.481.3813

Note Svc. Music, Canada 800.655.8863

Note Svc. Music, U.S. 800.628.1528

Percussion Express 815.229.3131

Steve Weiss Music 215.329.1639

World Music Institute 212.545.7536

PROGRAMS

ARTS-IN-EDUCATION

Ethos Percussion Group
PO Box 397 East Elmhurst NY 11369
P&F: 718.661.3334
Eml: ethos@earthlink.net
Web: http://home.earthlink.net/~
Dedicated to the advancement of the percussive arts in perf & educ. since 1990. One of Nth Americas most active touring perc. ensembles. Ethos has rcvd critical & popular acclaim for their concert workshops & educ. programs, has rlsd 3 recordings & offers a perf. video. Matching funding avail for outreach perf.s.

CLINICS & WORKSHOPS

Annual Djembe Institute 800.306.9033

Bands of America 800.848.Band

Berklee World Perc. Festival 617.266.1400

College Music Society
202 West Spruce St. Missoula, MT 59802
P: 800.729.0235 /406.721.9616 **F:** 406.721.9419
Eml: cms@music.org **Web:** http://www.music.org.

Drum Making Workshop 413.529.2319

Escola Nova de Samba 213.346.9336

Florida Drum Expo 813.889.3874

Kosa Int'l Percussion Workshop
P: 800.541.8401
Eml: kosa@istar.ca
Web: http://home.istar.ca/~kosa/homepage.htm
See ad opposite pg.

Mid-West Int'l Band & Orch. 847.729.4629

Modern Drummer Festival 201.239.4140

Montreal Drum Fest
P:514.928.1726 **F:** 514.670.8683
Produced by publishers of Musicien Quebecois & Drums Etc. Magazine, this is Canada's biggest drum festival. Takes place yearly in November. Call for more info. & exact dates. Also see ad on pg 179

Moonsisters Drum Camp for Womyn . 510.547.8386

EARN and **LIVE** an
ntire week with <u>THE
ARTISTS</u> that define
percussion for the
NEXT CENTURY

998 Annual
World
Percussion
woRkSHOp

KOSA

TERNATIONAL PERCUSSION WORKSHOPS

CULTY ALUMNI: DAVID GARIBALDI • GLEN VELEZ
DOM FAMULARO • IGNACIO BERROA
MICHAEL SPIRO • ALESSANDRA BELLONI
GORDON GOTTLIEB • *RÉPERCUSSION:*
[ALDO MAZZA • CHANTAL SIMARD
LUC LANGLOIS • ROBERT LÉPINE]
DELPHINE PAN DÉOUÉ • WILL CALHOUN
HORACEE ARNOLD

> find out more about the
1998 Event, please call

1-800-541-8401
e-mail: kosa@istar.ca
: http://home.istar.ca/~kosa/homepage.htm

PROGRAMS

CLINICS & WORKSHOPS

PASIC
PO Box 25 Lawton, OK 73502
P: 405.353.1455 **F:** 405.353.1456
Eml: percarts @pas.org
Web: http://www.pas.org
Largest "percussion only" show w/ 1000's of drummers / perc's, educators & music ind. professionals. Product exhibits, perf. & clinics. See ad pg 174.

Steel Band Workshop 304.293.5330x213

Tom Hannums Mobile Perc Seminars . 413.545.6060

Texas Bandmasters Assoc. 210.599.7585

Univ. N. Tex. Marching Drum Camp . 817.565.4124

Univ. N. Tex. Summer Drumset Camp . 817.565.3714

United States Percussion Camp . . 217.581.3925

World Rhythm Fest. & Days of Perc. . 206.548.0916

DRUM CIRCLES

California
Concord Community Drumming Circle
Concord 510.676.3151
Drum Circle- Palo Alto 415.493.8046
Spiritual Drum Circle - Los Gatos . . . 408.358.1212

Connecticut
Sono Drum Circle - Sth Norwalk   . .

Florida
Roots of Rhythm - Ft. Lauderdale .   954.566.9333

Georgia
Atlanta Community 404.633.4070
Drums Gathering 404.377.0764

Hawaii
Honolulu Community 803.777.Drum

Illinois
Chicago's Rhythm Revolution
Chicago 773.286.0605
Drum Circle - Deerfield 610.696.7433

Louisiana
Mystic Head of Nutrias - N. Orleans . 504.949.0369

Missouri
World Percussion - St. Louis 314.644.0235

New York
Womens Progressive- NYC 212.245.1488
Earthbeat - Long Island 516.421.5757

Pennsylvania
New Moon - West Redding 610.374.3730

Texas
African Drumming, Global Rhythms & Hippie Style
Drum Circle & Gatherings - Dallas . . .214.823.Drum
Psychedelic Drum Jam - Dallas . . . 214.363.0660
Spiritual / Men Only - Dallas 214.324.9495
Tribal Drum - Denton 817.381.2769

Washington
Seattle Community - Issaquah 206.391.5060

ORGANIZATIONS

CONVENTIONS

Int'l Assoc. of Jazz Educators 913.776.8744

International Drummers Meeting . . . 026.183.011

Mid-West Int'l Band & Orch. 847.729.4629

Music Educators Nat'l Conference . . 703.860.4000

P.A.S.I.C.
PO Box 25 Lawton, OK 73502
P: 405.353.1455 **F:** 405.353.1456
Eml: percarts @pas.org
Web: http://www.pas.org
Largest "percussion only" show w/ 1000's of drummers/ Perc's, educators & music ind. professionals. Prod. exhibits, perf. & clinics. See ad pg 139.

Texas Bandmasters Assoc. 210.599.7585

Texas Music Educ. Assoc. 512.452.0710

ORGANIZATIONS

Drum

All One Tribe - NM 505.751.0019

Circles of Harmony- VA 703.463.2650

Nat'l Drum Assoc. (NDA) 800.979.Drum

Perc. of N. India Development - .CA . . . 805.259.3195

Percussive Arts Society
PO Box 25 Lawton, OK 73502
P: 405.353.1455 **F:** 405.353.1456
Eml: percarts @pas.org
Web: http://www.pas.org
Membership Org. w/ publications & convention, dedicated to the educ. & promotion of all disciplines & styles of perc. See ad opposite pg 174.

Village Heartbeat - CA 415.493.8046

Drum & Dance

Djoniba Drum & Dance - NYC 212 477-3464

Earthdrum Council - MA 508.371.2502

Jobo Kunda - ME 207.422.9529

Earthbeat - NY 516.421.5757

ORGANIZATIONS

ORGANIZATIONS cont'd

General Music

Bands of America 800.848.Band

College Music Society
202 West Spruce St. Missoula, MT 59802
P: 800.729.0235 406.721.9616 **F:** 406.721.9419
Eml: cms@music.org **Web:** http://www.music.org
Professional Svc Org. Dedicated to gathering &
disseminating ideas on the philosophy of music
as an integral part of higher educ. See ad pg 170.

Mid-West Int'l Band & Orch. 847.729.4629

Music Educators Nat'l Conf.
(MENC) 703.860.4000

Seattle World Percussion Society . . . 206.548.0916

Texas Bandmasters Assoc. 210.599.7585

Texas Music Educ. 512.452.0710

World Music Institute 212.545.7536

Young Audiences (CA)
PO Box 55670 Valencia CA 91385
P: 805.259.3195 **F:** 805.259.3195

Young Audiences (NY)
115 E. 92 St. NYC, NY 10128
P: 212.831.8110
Web: http://www.youngaudiences.org
34 chapters & affil. organizations in 22 states working together to create comm. collaboration on behalf
of the arts & educ. Call for chapter near you.

Travel / Study

Caribbean Music & Dance 510.444.7173

Djoniba Drum & Dance 212.477.3464

Jobo Kunda 207.422.9529

Trade Resources

EVENTS

ORGANIZATIONS

PUBLICATIONS

TRADE RESOURCES

EVENTS

Drum

Florida Drum Expo 813.889.3874

Modern Drummer Festival
12 Old Bridge Rd. Cedar Grove, NJ 07009
P: 201.239.4140 **F:** 201.239.7139
Eml: moddrummer@aol.com
Web: http://www.moderndrummer.com
Yearly drum festival sponsored by Modern
Drummer magazine. Also see ad pg 185.

Montreal Drum Fest
439 Rue St. Helene Longueuil (Quebec) J4K 3R3
P: 514.928.1726 **F:** 514.670.8683
Largest yearly Canadian drum festival.
Sponsored by Musicien Quebecois Magazine/
Drums Etc. Magazine. Also See ad opp. pg.

International Drummers Meeting,
Koblenz 026.183.011

Percussive Arts Society (PASIC)
PO Box 25 Lawton, OK 73502
P: 405.353.1455 **F:** 405.353.1456
Eml: percarts @pas.org
Web: http://www.pas.org
Largest "percussion only" show w/ 1000's of drum-
mers/ Perc's, educators & music ind. professionals.
prod. exhibits, perf. & clinics. See ad pg 174.

General

Billboards Latin Amer. Music Conf. .. 212.536.5002

Canadian Music Week 416.695.9236

College Music Journal (CMJ) 516.466.6000

Doing Music & Nothing Else 800.448.3621

Frankfurt Musik Messe 404.984.8026

Int'l Assoc. of Jazz Educators 913.776.8744

JazzTimes Convention 301.588.4114

LASS Songwriters Expo 213.467.7823

Latin American Music Expo 914.993.0489

Music Educators Nat'l Conference 703.860.4000

Music West'96 .... 604.684.9338

NAMM (Summer) 800.767.Namm

NAMM (Winter) 800.767.Namm

Philadelphia Music Conference ... 215.426.4109

Texas Bandmasters Assoc. 210.599.7585

Ticketmaster Music Showcase ... 800.800.3232

West LA Music Expo 310.477.1945

SUBSCRIBE TO CANADA'S DRUM MAGAZINE

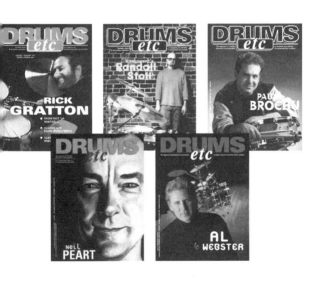

5 issues per year

ORGANIZATIONS

Drum

Nat'l Drum Assoc. (NDA) 800.979.drum

Percussion Mktng Council (PMC)
38 W. 21 St. 5flr NYC, NY 10010
P: 212.924.9175 **F:** 212.675.3577
Trade org. made up of manuf. & suppliers. PMC's goals are to expand the drum mkt by promoting drums & drumming as a positive, healthy activity for the public through activities & events.
See ad opposite pg.

Percussive Arts Society (PAS)
(See Events/ Drums for vitals)
Membership Org. w/ publications & convention, dedicated to the educ. & promotion of all disciplines & styles of perc. Also see ad pg 174.

General

Academy of Country Music 213.462.2351

Amer. Soc. of Comp, Authors & Publ.   212.621.6000

American Fed. of Musicians 212.869.1330

Austin Lawyers & Acct's for the Arts   512.338.4458

Austin Music Business Assoc. 512.288.1044

Black Arts Alliance 512.477.9660

Black Rock Coalition 212.713.5097

California Lawyers for the Arts 510.444.6351

California Lawyers for the Arts 415.775.7200

California Lawyers for the Arts 310.395.8893

Canadian Acad. of Recd.Arts 416.485.3135

Canadian Indie Record Prod. Assoc. 416.593.1665

Canadian Recording Industry 416.967.7272

College Music Society 800.729.0235

Country Music Assoc. 615.244.2840

Creative Resources Guild 310.285.3495

Cutting Edge Music Bus. Conf. . . . 504.945.1800

Florida Music Assoc. 813.988.6016

Gospel Music Assoc. 615.242.0303

Home Recording Rights Coalition . 800.282.tape

Houston Netwk of Lyricists & Songwriters
. . . . 713.264.4330

Ind. Music Producers Syndicate . . 800.677.8838

Int'l Assoc. of Jazz Educators 913.776.8744

Int'l Business Music Assoc 216.455.2800

Int'l Drum Month 212.924.9175

Be A Player!

This message brought to you by:

THE PERCUSSION MARKETING COUNCIL

ORGANIZATIONS cont'd

Jazz World Society	201.939.0836
Jazzmobile Inc.	212.866.4900
Lifebeat	212.245.3240
Long Island Songwriters Assoc.	516.338.5154
LA Songwriters Showcase	213.467.7823
Musicians Against Racism/Sexism (MARS)	212.685.Mars
Memphis Songwriters Assoc.	901.763.1957
Milwaukee Musicians Co-op	414.384.6596
Minnesota Music Academy	612.341.1777
Music Alliance	310.204.0827

Music Cares
3402 Pico Blvd. Santa Monica, CA 90405
P: 310.392.3777 **F:** 310.392.2188
Financial assistance grant program. Provides critical support to music prof. for rent, utilities, sustenance, medicine, medical treatment, drug treatment and other basic needs.

Music Distributors Assoc.	212.924.9175
Music Educators Nat'l Conference	703.860.4000
Musicians Against AIDS	415.252.7605
Musicians Contact Service	213.851.2333
Musicians National Referral	800.366.4447
Nashville Assoc. of Musicians Local 257	615.244.9514
Nat'l Acad.of Rec. Arts & Sciences	212.245.5440
Nat'l Acad.of Rec. Arts & Sciences	312.786.1121
Nat'l Acad.of Rec. Arts & Sciences	404.875.1440
Nat'l Acad.of Rec. Arts & Sciences	415.433.7112
Nat'l Acad.of Rec. Arts & Sciences	615.255.8777
Nat'l Acad.of Rec. Arts & Sciences	901.525.5500
Nat'l Acad.of Rec. Arts & Sciences	213.463.7178
Nat'l Acad.of Rec. Arts & Sciences	818.843.8253
Nat'l Assoc. of Indie Record Dist. & Mfrs.	609.482.8999
Nat'l Music Publishers Assoc.	212.370.5330
National Assoc. of Music Merchants (NAMM)	800.767.namm
N. CA Songwriters Assoc.	415.327.8296
NCSA Songwriter Conference	415.327.8296
New England Songwriters Assoc.	800.448.3621

TRADE RESOURCES

ORGANIZATIONS cont'd

New Music Seminar	212.473.4343
Nashville Songwriters Assoc.	615.256.3354
Pacific N.W. Songwriters Assoc.	206.824.1568
Percussive Marketing Council	212.924.9175
Professional Musicians Local 47	213.462.2161
Professional Musicians Referral	612.825.6848
Recording Musicians Assoc	213.462.4rma
Recording Ind. Assoc. of America	202.775.0101
San Diego Songwriters Guild	619.225.2131
Songwriters Assoc. of Wash.	301.654.8434
Songwriters of Wisconsin	414.733.9525
Southeastern Music	813.989.1472
Southern Songwriters Guild	318.949.0505
Southern VA Songwriters Assoc.	703.389.1525
Tennesee Songwriters Assoc.	615.824.4555
Texas Bandmasters Assoc.	210.599.7585
Women in Music Nt'l Ntwk	510.471.1752
Women's Indie Label Dist. Ntwk	517.323.4325

PUBLICATIONS

Drum

Batteur - France	01.40.35.73.73
Batterista- Italy	06.589.9018
Drum!	408.971.9794
Drum Business	201.239.4140

Drum Corps World
PO Box 8052 Madson, WI 57308-8052
P: 608.241.2292 **F:** 608.241.4974
Eml: DCWPub@AOL.com
The voice of the drum & Bugle corp activity
worldwide. Tabloid fomat. See ad opp. pg.

Drummer Dude 503.366.0481

Drums Etc.
439 Rue St. Helene Longueuil (Quebec) J4K 3R3
P: 514.928.1726 **F:** 514.670.8683
Canada's only drum magazine. Tailored to the needs
of the Canadian drum industry. Articles in both
French & English. Publishes 5x's per yr. Call for info.
Also see ad pg 177.

PUBLICATIONS Cont'd

Drum

Modern Drummer Publications
12 Old Bridge Rd. Cedar Grove, NJ 07009
P: 201.239.4140 **F:** 201.239.7139
Eml: moddrummer@aol.com
Web: http://www.moderndrummer.com
Monthly drum magazine See ad opposite pg.

Nashville Percussion Insider 615.313.9000

Not So Modern Drummer
500 Lafayette St. Nashville,TN 37210
P: 615.244.nsmd **F:** 615.244.6767
Eml: NSMDjohn@aol.com
Premiere vintage drum magazine. See ad below.

Percussion Source 212.253.8869

Percussioni - Italy 06.589.9018

Percussive Notes
PO Box 25 Lawton, OK 73502
P: 405.353.1455 **F:** 405.353.1456
Percussive Arts Society publication. See ad pg 174

PUBLICATIONS Cont'd

Drum

Rhythms - UK 01225.442244

SLAGWERKkrant - Netherlands . . . 020.675.5308

Stick It Magazine
3645 Jeanine Dr. ,Ste 201, CO Springs, CO 80917
P: 800.664.8482/ 719.637.3395 **F:** 719.737.3396
Eml: tgannaway@juno.com
Bi-monthly drum publication, inclusive of all facets
of drum & perc. fields. Each issue brings a companion cd. See ad pg 181.

Sticks and Mallets
20 Mellen St., Hopedale, MA 01747
P/ F: 508.634.9202

Sticks Magazine
Germany. . . . . 49(0)22 36.962170

Talking Drums
PO Box 1490 Severna, MD 21146
P: 410.544.7894 **F:** 410.345.8060
Eml: Talkdrums@usa.pipeline.com
Quarterly drum & perc. magazine. See ad pg. 189.

Drum & Dance

Rhythm Music Magazine
928 Broadway Suite 1206, NYC NY 10010
P: 617.497.0356 **F:** 212.253.8892
See ad opp. pg.

General

Agent & Mgr. Facilities Mag 212.532.4150

Agents Inc. 617.277.4435

BAM 510.934.3700

BAM South 213.851.8600

Billboard 212.764.7300

Billboard CA 213.525.2300

Canadian Musician 905.641.3471

College Music Journal (CMJ) 516.466.6000

Concert Circuit 713.277.6626

Contemporary Christian Music . . . 615.386.3011

Country Music 203.221.4950

Creative Drum Magazine 516.475.8476

TRADE RESOURCES

PUBLICATIONS Cont'd

Creem 212.647.0222
Crunchy Music Stuff 910.230.0201
Down Beat 630.941.2030
Electronic Musician 510.653.3307
Gig Magazine 818.797.4544
Gigging Musician - UK 01954.789888
Hits Magazine . . . .
818.501.7900Illinois Entertainer . . . 312.922.9333
Jazz Times 609.486.1122
Jazziz Magazine 904.375.3705
LA Jazz Scene 818.504.2115
Latin Beat 310.516.6767
MIX 510.653.3307
Music Business Int'l 212.779.1212
Music Connection 818.755.0101
Music Inc. 630.941.2030
Music Merchandise Review (MMR) . . 617.964.5100
Music Paper/Musician's Exchange . . 212.614.0300
Music Scene International 805.944.3020
Musician 212.536.5208

Musicien Magazine
439 Rue St. Helene Longueuil (Quebec) J4K 3R3
P: 514.928.1726 **F:** 514.670.8683
Premiere Canadian music magazine. Sponsor of
Canada's biggest drum festival. See ad pg 177.

Musico Pro 303.516.9118
New England Performer 617.279.1200
NY Latino 718.657.8248
Official Country Music Directory . . 619.322.3858
Pennsylvania Musician Magazine . 717.444.2423
Performance Magazine 817.338.9444
Recording Magazine 619.738.5571
Reggae Report Int'l Magazine 305.933.1178
Rhythm Music Magazine 617.497.0356
Rhythm & News Magazine 914.463.3040
Rolling Stone 212.484.1616
School Music Dealer 310.456.5812
The Aquarian Weekly 201.783.4346
The Beat Magazine 213.257.2328
The Nashville Scene 615.244.7989
The Performing Songwriter 615.297.6972

HEALTH

PROFESSIONAL

PROMOTION

TRAVEL

services

MISC. SERVICES

HEALTH

Doc's Proplugs, Inc. 408 462.5919

House Ear Institute / HIP Program
2100 West 3rd Street 5th flr, Los Angeles CA 90057
P: 213.483.4431 **F:** 213.483.8789
For more info on protecting your hearing call "HIP"
"Hearing is Priceless"or write for free ear filters.

Musicians Pharmacy Rx - In Design Mfg
21 Willets Dr., Syossett NY 11791
P/ F: 516.364.6611
Health products designed exclusively for musi-
cians. Including Pro-Techt, recommended for
CTS & Arthritis sufferers.

PROFESSIONAL SVCS

Cd Manufactures/Dupe

A to Z Music Services, Inc. 212.260.0237

Alshire Custom Service 213.849.4671

Audio Cassette Duplicator Co. . . . 818.762.acdc

CD House One Stop 213.969.0908

CD Labs 818.505.9581

Compact Disc Service 818.241.9103

Imperial Tape Company 310.396.2008

Mediaworks Int'l 615.327.9114

Omni Source 800.668.0098

Prophet Disc Mfg. 800.491.8141

Quality Clones 213.464.5853

Rainbo Records & Cassettes 310.829.3476

Tape Specialty, Inc. 818.786.6111

Tom Parham Audio 714.871.1395

Cd/ Video Dupe

Abbey Tapes 800.257.best

Cd/ Video Production

American Sound & Video Corp. . . . 810.795.1900

World Audio/Video Enterp 800.777.1927

Management

Management Consultants 213.461.0757

MISC. SERVICES

PROFESSIONAL SVCS

Referral Services

Musicians Nat'l Referral 800.366.4447

Professional Musicians Referral . . . 612.825.6848

Studio A Booking & Referral Srvce . . 615.320.9394

Studio Referral Service 818.508.8828

PROMOTION

Design Services

Robert Chi
P: 212.686.9657
Esoteric fukt-up conceptual design &/ or fuzzy
grainy photo illustrations from a media-maniac.

Kick Ass Design
423 Atlantic Ave. Ste 3E Brooklyn, NY 11217
P: 718.875.6353 F: 718.875.5586
Maria Casini: advertising, design & illustration.
15 years design experience.

Photo Dupe

ABC Pictures 417.869.3456

Duplicate Photo and Imaging 213.466.7544

Photography

Paul Norman Photography L.A. . . .310.392.1421

Melanie Weiner Photography
219 Court St. Brooklyn, NY 11201
P: 718.330.0358 Experienced Portrait & Band
Photographer, Subjects range from to Christie Hynde
to Sound Garden.

Printing

Modern Postcard 800.959.8365

Standard Deluxe T-shirt Co. 800. 382.9473

Urban Images 718.875.4219

MISC. SERVICES

TRAVEL

Agent

Maria Pollio / Kea World Travel
264 Closter Dock Rd Closter, NJ 07624
P: 800.453.6589/ 201.768.3600
Complete travel svcs. 32 yrs. exp. Svc clients from
all areas of U.S. Call Toll Free 9-5pm EST

MARIA POLLIO

32yrs. experience
Personal Travel Services
Domestic/Int'l,
Kea World Travel

800.453.6589
201.768,3600

Airline

Aer Lingus	800.223.6537
Aero Peru	800.777.7717
Aerolineas Argentinas	800.333.0276
Aeromexico	800.237.6639
Air Afrique	800.456.9192
Air Aruba	800.882.7822
Air Canada	800.776.3000
Air France	800.237.2747
Air India	212.751.6200
Air Jamaica	800.523.5585
Air L.A.	800.933.5952
Air New Zealand	800.262.1234
Alaska Airlines	800.426.0333
Alitalia Airlines	800.223.5730
Alm Antillean Airlines	800.327.7230

MISC. SERVICES

TRAVEL cont'd

Aloha Airlines	800.367.5250
America West	800.235.9292
American Airlines	800.433.7300
Austrian Airlines	800.843.0002
Avianca Airlines	800.284.2622
Bahamas Air	800.222.4262
British Airways	800.247.9297
BWIA Int'l-British West Indies Air	800.538.2942
Canadian Airlines Int'l	800.426.7000
Cathay Pacific Airways	800.233.2742
China Airlines	800.227.5118
Continental Airlines	800.525.0280
Delta Air Lines	800.221.1212
Egyptair	800.334.6787
El Al Israel Airlines	800.223.6700
Finnair	800.950.5000
Hawaiian Airlines	800.367.5320
Horizon Air	800.547.9308
Iberia Airlines	800.772.4642
Icelandair	800.223.5500
Japan Air Lines	800.525.3663
Kenya Airways	212.681.1200
Kiwi International Airlines	800.538.5494
KLM Royal Dutch Airlines	800.374.7747
Korean Air Lines	800.438.5000
L.A.N. Chile Airlines	800.735.5526
Lufthansa Airlines	800.645.3880
Malaysia Airlines	800.421.8641
Mexicana Airlines	800.531.7921
Midwest Express Airlines	800.452.2022
Northwest Airlines	800.225.2525
Olympic Airways	212.838.3600
Pakistan Int'l Airlines	212.370.9156
Philippine Airlines	800.435.9725

misc.
195
svcs.

TRAVEL cont'd

Qantas Airways	800.227.4500
Reno Air	800.736.6247
S.A.S./Scandinavian Airlines System	800.221.2350
Sabena Belgian World Airlines	800.955.2000
Singapore Airlines	800.742.3333
South African Airways	800.722.9675
Southwest Airlines	800.435.9792
Swissair	800.221.4750
Tap Air Portugal	800.221.7370
Thai Airways Int'l	800.426.5204
Tower Air	800.221.2500
TWA	800.221.2000
U.S. Air	800.428.4322
United Airlines	800.241.6522
Varig Brazilian Airlines	800.468.2744
VIASA/ Venezuelan Int'l Airways	800.468.4272
Virgin Atlantic Airways	800.862.8621

Car Rental

A.B.C. Car Rental	800.736.8148
Advantage Rent-a-Car	800.777.5500
Alamo Rent-a-Car	800.327.9633
Avis Rent-a-Car	800.331.1212
Budget Rent-a-Car	800.527.0700
Dollar Rent-a-Car	800.800.4000
Enterprise Rent-a-Car	800.325.8007
Hertz Rent-a-Car	800.654.3131
National Inter Rent	800.328.4567
Payless Car Rentals	800.729.5377
Practical Rent-a-Car	800.426.5243
Rent-a-Wreck	800.535.1391
Thrifty Car Rental	800.367.2277
U.S.A. Rent-a-Car	800.777.9377
Ugly Duckling Rent-a-Car	800.843.3825
Value Rent-a-Car	800.327.2501

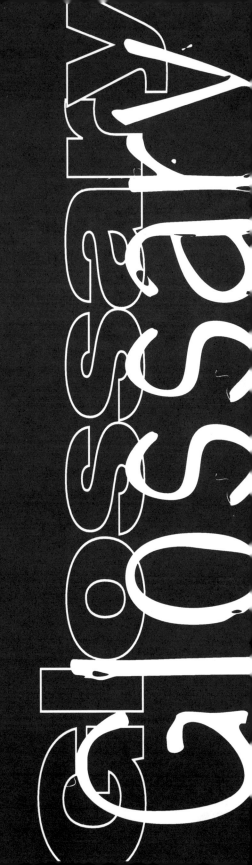

Glossary

GLOSSARY

Ashiko Is a narrow conical shaped wood drum, of African origin. It is rope tuned and usually has a goatskin head. It can also be made of synthetic materials and heads. **Mfr. Source ideas:** Afena Akoma, Africa West, African & World Perc, AV Drumworks, Bailes, Drum Bros., Everyones Drumming, LJ Percussion, LP Music, Remo, Taos

Afuché (a-fu-shay) Also known as a cabasa, the Afuché is made of endless loops of plated steel ball chain. These loops surround a textured stainless steel cylinder enclosed by smoothly finished flanges and joined with a handle. The cylinder is placed in the palm of the hand while the hand on the handle twists back and forth causing the steel ball chain to rub against the textured cylinder, giving a rhythmic scraping effect. **Mfr. Source ideas:** LP Music

Agogo Bell Popular in Brazillian samba rhythms, agogo bells are made up of 2 attached conical shaped bells, one slightly lower pitch than the other. They are played with a stick and some can also be pressed together to create an additional rhythm when the bells meet. **Mfr. Source ideas:** LP Music

Bata Drum This hour glass shaped drum is a traditional ceremonial drum used in the "Santeria Religion". It is a 2 headed drum which tapers in diameter on one end. Bata drums come in three sizes. The Iya (lg), Omele or Itotole (med), and Oncocolo (sml). Sometimes a donut shaped piece of modeling clay is used on the large head of the Iya (lg) drum in order to dampen the pitch. It is played with both hands on each side of the drum. **Mfr. Source ideas:** Caribbean Rhythms, LP Music

Berimbau (bear-im-bow) Traditionally found in Africa & Brazil , the berimbau consists of a bow made of wood, strung with steel wire, with a resonating gourd attached. Played by striking the string with the stick while fretting the string with a coin and holding a shaker. **Mfr. Source ideas:** LP Music

Bomba Drums These Folklore drums originated in Puerto Rico. Often made of rum barrel oak with natural hides. **Mfr. Source ideas:** Caribbean Rythms

Bongos These drums are of Cuban origin. In Latin music they are typically played sitting down, held between the knees. In pop settings they can be seen played on a stand. Traditionally they are made of wood but can also be found in fiberglass. The small head is known as the "Macho" (male) and the large head is known as the "Hembra" (female).

Mfr. Source ideas: Caribbean Rhythms, LP Music, Matthew Congas, Remo

Cajon The Cajon (box), origi- nates from the Andean mountain region of South America. It is basically a wooden box, and is played by sitting on top and rock- ing the bottom edge on & off the ground while hand drumming on the front. When the center is hit, it produces a broad deep tone which is projected from a hole in the back. Some cajons have a loose top front panel, which when played on the top edges give off a high pitch rattle to simulate a snare sound. **Mfr. Source ideas:** LP Music

Cajun /Zydeco Rib Boards These look like a corrugat- ed vest of armor. Rubbing against the ridges gives gives a very rhytmic scraping sound much like a guiro.

Castanets Castanets are wooden clappers typi- cally used by Spanish Flamenco dancers. They are traditionally played in the hand, but can also be found attached to a handle or base for faster playing in different music style settings. **Mfr. Source ideas:** LP Music

Caxixi (ka-she-she) & **Ganza** Shakers are both similar in that they are woven shakers filled with loose beads (like maracas). The caxixi is bell shaped with a looped handle and a resillient bottom panel for accenting when shaken. The Ganza is cylindrical and has a resillienttop and bottom for a louder, high pitched sound. **Mfr. Source ideas:** Lawton Percussion, LP Music, Rhythms

Clave Sticks These are 2 short wooden sticks that are struck together to give a sharp crack. The African style clave usually has one thicker stick with a scooped out center which allows for sound variation. They can be made of exotic woods or synthetic materials. Clave is a fundamental sound in most Latin music. The rhythm associated with these stick is also known as the "clave" and is in a 3/2 or 2/3 feel.
Mfr. Source ideas: Caribbean Rhythms, LP Music

Cog Rattle Winding the handle of the cog rattle makes the cog strike the wooden tongues with a loud clatter. Beethoven used a cog rattle to simulate rifle fire in his Battle Symphony.

Conga Drums With its origin in African & Cuban tradition, Conga drums are probably the most popular hand drums today. They come in a variety of woods as well as fiberglass, and are available in different sizes and countours. The Superquinto or Requinto is the smallest, usually 9" in diameter, the Quinto 11", the Conga 11 3/4" and the Tumba 12 1/2". These sizes are standard but other sizes can be found. **Mfr. Source ideas:** Caribbean Rhythms, LP Music, Remo

Cuica (kwee-ka) The cuica is a small, cylindrical, metal friction drum. It is a staple of Brazillian Samba schools. It is played by rubbing a wet cloth to a thin bamboo stick that is tied under a goatskin head, and applying pressure to the head for pitch variation. This produces an almost vocal like sound.
Mfr. Source ideas: LP Music, Remo

Darbuka The Darbuka is goblet shaped --single-headed drum. It is popular in Arab countries and is the cousin to the Turkish doumbeck. The base is made of a solid piece of aluminum or nickel and can come engraved or with material covering. **Mfr. Source ideas:** LP Music, Tribe of Kings (ceramic)

Didgeridoo Is a unique instrument from the Aboriginal culture in Austrailia. Traditional didgeri-

doos are most often made from termite hollowed branches of eucalyptus. Circular breathing creates a haunting sound resonating with ancient wisdom.
Mfr. Source ideas: Blu Roo Ridgy, Boongar Arts

Djembe (jem-bay) The djembe is a goblet shaped, single headed drum of African origin. It is traditionally rope tuned but can also be found with mechanical tuning. The head is made of thin goatskin. The djembe's shape produces crackling highs and incredible bass tones.
Mfr. Source ideas: Afena Akoma, AV Drumworks, Bailes, Everyones Drumming, L.J. Percussion, LP Music, Remo, Taos

Djun Djun Traditionally played with Djembes and Ashiko drums featuring all welded metal hoops, natural wood or African cloth covering, traditional rope tension with natural shaved goat skin heads and made of cherry wood. **Mfr. Source ideas:** Afena, AV Drumworks, Bailes, Everyones Drumming, Drum Bros., Remo

Doumbeck A small goblet shaped Turkish drum with a base made of metal or ceramic and a goatskin head. It is played with the fingers and hand. One hand can be placed inside the base to vary the pitch.
Mfr. Source ideas: Barb Lund, Clay Soundscapes (Tygart), Full Circle, LP Music, Remo

Drum Set (See next page)

Ewe Barrel Drum Drums of the Ewe speaking people of Africa are made of staved poplar. Skin is stretched across the mouth of the drum and pulled taut by a durable rope and peg tuning system. Ewe barrel drums are constructed in various sizes which articulate the function and character of each drum in the ensemble. The drums are played upright, tilted or suspended in a stand. Played with sticks or hands, they produce a variety of distinct projecting tones.

DRUMSET (BASIC KIT)

(A) Bass Drum This large drum lies on its side and is played by foot with a felt-covered beater connected to a bass drum pedal. It comes in different depths and sizes and gives a short deep thud.

(B) Bass Drum Pedal is a steel footplate with beater attached. When stepped on, the beater strikes against the center of the bass drum. With add'tl attachments pedals can also be used to hit bells, blocks & tamborines.

(C) Cymbals Cymbals are made of bronze & come in many different variations. 1. Crash (loud) 2. Ride (center bell for pinging sound), 3. Splash (small, bright sounding) 4. China (upturned edge). They come in different sizes & thickness' which determine how bright or dark the sound will be.

(D) Floor Tom This is a large self standing tom-tom. It usually comes with 3 legs and stands on its own. It can also be held on a rack or seperate stand. Its gives off a deep, resonant note that falls in between the mounted tom-toms and the bass drum.

(E) Hi-Hat This is a pair of cymbals mounted on a stand. Pressing the pedal closes them with a short clash.

(F) Snare Drum Across the base of this drum is a set of wires called the snare. Striking the drum causes the snare to vibrate against the lower head, or the skin, adding a sharp crack to the sound of the drum.

(G) Tom-Toms "Tom-toms", or "toms," are mounted on the top of the bass drum. These small drums give high - medium pitched, mellow notes.

Mfr. Source ideas: Drumset- African American, Chris Brady, DW, Giannini, Mapex, Remo, Rocket, Woodstock, Taos. **Cymbals**- UFIP. **Bass Drum Pedals**- Airlogic Percussion, Axis, DW, Mapex

Flexatone The flexatone has a thin metal sheet to which steel springs with a round knob is affixed. Shaking the instrument makes the knob hit the sheet, which gives a high wailing sound. Bending the sheet changes the pitch of the sound.
Mfr. Source ideas: LP Music,

Frame Drums There are many different origins for frame drums, from Celtic to Native American. They are all similar in that they are all single headed hand drums, like large tambourine (w/o the jingles). The "Bodhran" is of Irish origin, made with a traditional goat skin head, hardwood crossbraces, laminated hardwood shell and played with a wooden beater. **Mfr. Source ideas:** All One Tribe (Nat. Amer.), Remo, Taos (Nat. Amer.), Buck Musical (Bodhran).

Gourd Guiros Traditional style guiros are made of oblong shaped hollow gourds with carved ridges in the front and 2 finger holes in the back. Some are open ended on the top and some are completely enclosed. They are traditionally used in Latin music and are played with a wood or plastic stick to create a percussive scrape-like effect. **Mfr. Source ideas:** Caribbean Rhythms, Lawton, LP Music

Maracas Maracas are pairs of rattles that originate from South America. They are traditionally made of hollow gourds containing loose seeds, but modern maracas are typically found made of wood, leather or synthetic materials, and filled with beads or other similar filling. They come in pairs with a high/ low pitch variation. **Mfr. Source ideas:** Caribbean Rhythms, Lawton, LP Music, Remo

Marching Drum Marching drums are typically used in drum & bugle corp. performance. The drums are carried on a sling around the body so that the drummer can walk and play at the same time. The Snare drum is typically a much deeper shell than traditional drumset snares, and the head is tuned very taut. **Mfr. Source ideas:** Remo

Palo Drum These folkloric drums originated in the Dominican Republic. They are the predecessor to the tambora for rythms such as "gaga." Theycome in three sizes and are made of pine and natural cowskins. The serious gaga player will appreciate and value their "exotic" quality.
Mfr. Source ideas: Caribbean Rhythms

Planera Drum From Puerto Rico these drums are hand held tunable frame drums in which bomba and plena beats are frequently performed in Latin music. The shells are mahogany and have goatskin heads. They are easy to hold since traditional music is performed for long periods of time. This is a great drum to bring to a drum circle.
Mfr. Source ideas: Caribbean Rhythms

Pueblo Drums (American Indian) Pueblo Drums are carved from a solid log, with raw hide skins on both sides and rawhide lacing in-between. Wonderful deep tone! (The deeper and wider the drum, the deeper the sound.)
Mfr. Source ideas: Taos

Rainstick Rainsticks are traditionally made of cactus but can be found made with different materials including plastic. There is a series of toothpick like spines inside the cactus that criss cross, throughout the length of the rainstick causing the enclosed pebbles to bounce when rotated, giving off a rainlike sound effect. **Mfr. Source ideas:** LP Music

GLOSSARY

Shekeres (she-ke-ray) Traditionally from Africa, shekeres are gourds covered with a woven, beaded webbing, combining the three different elements of shaker, rattle and drum. They are shaken, twisted and hit on their bottom side to produce deep, resonant bass notes. Shekeres can now be found made of durable synthetic materials.
Mfr. Source ideas: Bailes, CaribbeanRhythms, Lawton, LP Music, Rhythms

Steel drums Originally fashioned from discarded 55 gallon oil drums by the 'panmen' of Trinidad in the mid 1940's. Popular throughout the Caribbean and in many other areas of the world, including the US. By varying the size of the notes on the top and the depth of the drum, the sounds range from a xylophone / piano combination to a resonance resembling violas and cellos beginning with a percussive beat. Typically played with mallets. **Mfr. Source ideas:** Fancy Pans, Lawton, Trinidad Tobago Drums

Surdo IThe surdo is played in conjunction with other Brazilian drums to deliver a great fundamental beat. **Mfr. Source ideas:** LP Music, Remo

Tabla Drums The se traditional cerimonial drums from India., are a pair of small drums, played in a sitting position on the floor. The larger round drum (bahya) is made of metal, and the taller narrower drum (tabla) is made of wood. They sit on two round (donut like) bases, covered in fabric.
Mfr. Source ideas: Ali Akbar, LP Music

G L O S S A R Y

Talking Drum Originally from Africa the talking drum is a 2 headed drum, with an hour glass shape. Both heads are the same size and are strung by rope. They are called "talking drums" because they can produce a wide range of pitches including high female sounds and low male sounds by squeezing the drums under the arm, while striking one of the heads with the hand or curved stick. **Mfr. Source ideas:** Afena Akoma, Africa West, LP Music

Tambora Originating from the Dominican Republic, the tambora is used in traditional fast paced Merengue music. It is a small, stocky looking, two headed drum, traditionally rope tuned but can be found with modern tuning lugs. It is played with the hand on one side and a wood beater or stick on the other. Some also come with a wood or synthetic block attached to the shell so the shell can be played and not damaged. **Mfr. Source ideas:** Caribbean Rhythms, LP Music

Thumb Piano Also known as a kalimba or mbira, the thumb pianos is of African origin. It consist of small, thin metal tongues of various lengths and when played with your thumbs, create a melodic piano like sound. The tongues may be mounted on a flat wood board, a hollow wood box or a hollow gourd. **Mfr. Source ideas:** LP Music

Timbales Made of stainless steel and brass, these drums have a lively sound. When you strike the side of the shell, it's called "cascara", the the driving force in Salsa music. Although originally only played in Latin music, Timbales are incorporated in all areas of music today. **Mfr. Source ideas:** LP Music, Remo

Timpani Also known as a **Kettle drum** is traditionally found in concert percussion settings. The kettle is copper or fiberglass and the head can be calfskin or synthetic. The pedal stretches varies the pitch.

Tongue Drums Also known as African slit 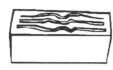 drums, are wooden boxes with slits cut on top. The "Tongues" are randomly pitched and have a very unique sound. This instrument is played with a mallet.

Mfr. Source ideas: Rhythms, Tapo Rhythm and Music

UDU Drums The UDU is a clay pot drum originating from Africa. ("Udu" means "pot") It has a side hole which, when the bass is hit, produces deep, haunting tones. They were initially used in religious and cultural ceremonies.
Mfr. Source ideas: LP Music, Rhythms, UDU Drums

 **Waterphones** A Waterphone is a monolithic, stainless steel and bronze tonal-friction instrument utilizing water in its resonator. Its sound has been compared to the haunting melodies of the humpback whale. Held by the neck or suspended by a cord, the Waterphone can be played with a bow, mallets or by hand.

Xylophone & Marimbas The xylophone & marimba are of African origin. They can be described as a piano keyboard on a stand, played with mallets. They differ in tonal range, with the Marimba being lower. The keys are different lengths & are usually made of rosewood, but can also be made of synthetics & other alternative materials including glass or stone. They contain hollow metal tubes (gourds on more traditional instruments) below the keys. These  are called resonators & help shape the sound.
Mfr. Source ideas: Marimba One (Concert), Rhythms (traditional)

XL 100% Cotton T's • Only $15
Specify Style A (Blk or Wht Shirt) or Style B (Blk only)
Please add $5 for S/H • NY State residents add $8\frac{1}{4}$ sales tax

Full Name

Address

City   **State**   **Zip Code**

Phone   **E-Mail**

- -

Full Name

Address

City   **State**   **Zip Code**

Phone   **E-Mail**

- -

Full Name

Address

City   **State**   **Zip Code**

Phone   **E-Mail**

- -

Full Name

Address

City   **State**   **Zip Code**

Phone   **E-Mail**

Full Name

Address

City   State   Zip Code

Phone   E-Mail

Full Name

Address

City   State   Zip Code

Phone   E-Mail

Full Name

Address

City   State   Zip Code

Phone   E-Mail

Full Name

Address

City   State   Zip Code

Phone   E-Mail

Full Name

Address

City   **State**   **Zip Code**

Phone   **E-Mail**

- -

Full Name

Address

City   **State**   **Zip Code**

Phone   **E-Mail**

- -

Full Name

Address

City   **State**   **Zip Code**

Phone   **E-Mail**

- -

Full Name

Address

City   **State**   **Zip Code**

Phone   **E-Mail**

 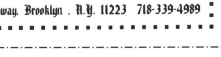

Full Name

Address

City   State   Zip Code

Phone   E-Mail

Full Name

Address

City   State   Zip Code

Phone   E-Mail

Full Name

Address

City   State   Zip Code

Phone   E-Mail

Full Name

Address

City   State   Zip Code

Phone   E-Mail

Full Name

Address

City **State** **Zip Code**

Phone **E-Mail**

Full Name

Address

City **State** **Zip Code**

Phone **E-Mail**

Full Name

Address

City **State** **Zip Code**

Phone **E-Mail**

Full Name

Address

City **State** **Zip Code**

Phone **E-Mail**

Full Name

Address

City   State   Zip Code

Phone   E-Mail

Full Name

Address

City   State   Zip Code

Phone   E-Mail

Full Name

Address

City   State   Zip Code

Phone   E-Mail

Full Name

Address

City   State   Zip Code

Phone   E-Mail

AREA CODES

Code	Location	Code	Location
201	New Jersey	403	Alberta Canada
202	Dist. of Columbia	404	Georgia
203	Connecticut	405	Oklahoma
204	Manitoba, Canada	406	Montana
205	Alabama	407	Florida
206	Washington	408	California
207	Maine	409	Texas
208	Idaho	410	Maryland
209	California	412	Pennsylvania
210	Texas	413	Massachussets
212	New York City	414	Wisconsin
213	California	416	Ont Canada
214	Texas	417	Missouri
215	Pennsylvania	418	Qbc Canada
216	Ohio	419	Ohio
217	Illinois	423	Tennessee
218	Minnesota	443	Maryland
219	Indiana	501	Arkansas
240	Maryland	502	Kentucky
248	Michigan	503	Oregon
250	BC Canada	504	Louisiana
301	Maryland	505	New Mexico
302	Delaware	506	NB Canada
303	Colorado	507	Minnesota
304	W. Virginia	508	Massachussets
306	Canada	509	Washington
307	Wyoming	510	California
308	Nebraska	512	Texas
309	Illinois	513	Ohio
310	California	514	Qbc Canada
312	Illinois	516	New York
313	Michigan	515	Iowa
314	Missouri	517	Michigan
315	New York	518	New York
316	Kansas	519	Ont Canada
317	Indiana	520	Arizona
318	Louisiana	540	Virginia
319	Iowa	541	Oregon
320	Minnesota	561	Florida
330	Ohio	562	California
334	Alabama	573	Missouri
352	Florida	601	Mississippi
360	Washington	602	Arizona
401	Rhode Island	603	New Hampshire
402	Nebraska	604	BC Canada

AREA CODES

605	S. Dakota	804	Virginia
606	Kentucky	805	California
607	New York	806	Texas
608	Wisconsin	807	Ont Canada
609	New Jersey	808	Hawaii
610	Pennsylvania	809	USVI/ Caribbean
612	Minnesota	810	Michigan
613	Ont Canada	812	Indiana
614	Ohio	813	Florida
615	Tennessee	814	Pennsylvania
616	Michigan	815	Illinois
617	Massachussets	816	Missouri
618	Illinois	817	Texas
619	California	818	California
626	California	819	Qbc Canada
630	Illinois	847	Illinois
701	N. Dakota	860	Connecticut
702	Nevada	864	S. Carolina
703	Virginia	870	Arkansas
704	N. Carolina	901	Tennessee
705	Ont Canada	902	Nova Scotia
706	Georgia	903	Texas
707	California	904	Florida
708	Illinois	905	Ont Canada
709	New Foundland	906	Michigan
712	Iowa	907	Alaska
713	Texas	908	New Jersey
714	California	909	California
715	Wisconsin	910	N. Carolina
716	New York	912	Georgia
717	Pennsylvania	913	Kansas
718	New York City	914	New York
719	Colorado	915	Texas
732	New Jersey	916	California
734	Michigan	918	Oklahoma
760	California	919	N. Carolina
770	Georgia	941	Florida
773	Illinois	954	Florida
781	Massachussetts	970	Colorado
787	Puerto Rico	972	Texas
801	Utah	973	New Jersey
802	Vermont	978	Massachussetts
803	S. Carolina		

AD INDEX

A D I N D E X

AD INDEX

N O T E S